Make It with Style
SLIPCOVERS

Make It with Style
SLIPCOVERS

Donna Lang

WITH JUDY PETERSEN

PHOTOGRAPHY BY GEORGE ROSS
ILLUSTRATIONS BY JOAN MULLIN

Clarkson Potter/Publishers
New York

With sincere thanks and appreciation to all those who contributed so generously to this book, especially Tiina Dodenhoff for keeping me on schedule and laughing; George Ross and associates for photographing with a magic lens; Judy Petersen for sewing so beautifully and instructing so accurately; Joan Mullin for illustrating so artistically; Chester Herbert, Shirley Westcott, Casey Pervis, and Mavis Brown for cutting slipcovers so expertly; Mary and John Hash, Madeline and Ian Hooper, Alexis and Jim Roiter for being such extraordinary clients and for graciously allowing us to photograph their homes; Pam Krauss, Susan Ginsberg, and Susan Voigt-Reising for their inspired guidance; Murray Douglas, Dean Rorvig, Margie Ford, Catherine Hanscom, Catherine Horton, Amy Krieger, and Manny Konigsberg for their beautiful fabrics and trims; and Mommy, Bill, Joe, Wes, and Keith for loving and supporting me so unconditionally.

Published by Clarkson N. Potter/Publishers, 201 East 50th Street, New York, New York 10022. Member of the Crown Publishing Group.

Random House, Inc. New York, Toronto, London, Sydney, Auckland

www.randomhouse.com

CLARKSON N. POTTER, POTTER, and colophon are trademarks of Clarkson N. Potter, Inc.

Printed in Hong Kong

Design by Andrzej Janerka

Library of Congress Cataloging-in-Publication Data
Lang, Donna.
Make it with style—slipcovers / by Donna Lang.
1. Slipcovers. I. Title.
TT395.L36   1998   97-42918
746.9'5—dc21   CIP

ISBN 0-517-88241-8

10 9 8 7 6 5 4 3 2 1

First Edition

PREVIOUS PAGE: *A traditional Louis XIV–style chair was customized with tie-on covers that repeat the color and lattice pattern of the walls. Complete directions for creating this quilted cover are on page 67.* OPPOSITE: *Piping cut on the bias from a miniature plaid print outlines the bow detailing on a chintz folding chair cover.*

Contents

Introduction

In my interior design business, I have found slipcovers to be true miracle workers of home decorating. They revitalize existing furniture at a reasonable price, hide a host of ills, and help keep decor in sync with the seasons. But perhaps the most exciting benefit of slipcovers is the one least touted: their potential for expressing creativity.

Some people can build a piece of furniture from scratch, others can upholster it for a lovely result—but the skills and tools required are many. Yet anyone possessing basic sewing skills, a bit of patience, and an inventive spirit can create slipcovers that will transform that furniture. The key? The innovative (and fun!) use of fabrics, trims, and closures.

The information and projects included in this book are designed to help slipcoverers of all experience levels create good-looking, well-fitted slipcovers for a wide range of furniture, from a simple upholstered chair to a traditional wing chair to a contemporary butterfly chair—and a great deal in between. But what I hope sets this book apart from other slipcover guides is the focus on *detail*. For example, that ordinary wing chair becomes extraordinary when covered with a slipcover made from a quilt with spaghetti tie bows as a closure (see page 71). And that butterfly chair cover becomes an exotic focal point when fabricated in a zebra-print canvas lined with red—and edged with pinked green felt.

To make this book as useful as possible, I've structured it to provide as much or as little information as you will need, depending on your experience level and interests.

• If you're a novice slipcoverer, read Part 1, "Before You Begin," and Part 2, "Creating Slipcovers," where I'll acquaint you with my approach to slipcovering by working step-by-step through the process for a basic chair. My experience has proven this approach to be the fastest, easiest method. It emphasizes smart, time-effective planning and construction aided by my professionally tested charts, formulas, and techniques. You'll also find a wealth of trim and embellishment suggestions to make your slipcover unique. Then browse through Part 3 for what I hope you'll agree is an enticing array of one-of-a-kind ideas, including step-by-step instructions for many of the projects pictured.

• If your slipcovering experience places you at an intermediate level, familiarize yourself with the methods and detail options in Part 2 (referring back to Part 1 as suggested). Chances are you'll find techniques that will save you time or frustration and delightful details that will add interest to your designs. Then look to Part 3 for a host of special projects for consideration—or inspiration.

A simple natural-cotton canvas slipcover for a slipper chair is accented with contrast-colored canvas welting and a bold cotton band trim around the skirt hem. The separate back pillows are embellished with appliquéd baskets of full-blown flowers that were cut from the allover floral print used elsewhere in the room. See page 102 for information on the appliqué technique.

• If you're an experienced slipcoverer, I hope the many photographs and unique details in this book provide a fresh and lively perspective that inspires you in your own slipcover designs.

• Whatever your skill level, you'll find helpful definitions of the terms that appear in bold-face; the definitions start on page 100. (In addition, you'll find definitions related to fabric on pages 16–18 and definitions related to trim on pages 24–28.)

• If you don't have the time, sewing skills, or inclination to make your own slipcovers, this book will prove a valuable asset in commissioning slipcovers through a professional. Browse for ideas, check the handy charts for yardage and trim estimates, consider the embellishments—and imagine the possibilities.

Whether you need to work a miracle or simply want to make an artful change to a piece of furniture, you'll find ideas for devising great-looking slipcovers that are as unique as your personal style.

Before You Begin

Before you make one cut or pin a single pin, you must plan your slipcover. Careful visualization and decision making now will help ensure the best results later. In this section, you'll find guidelines for choosing the right furniture piece to cover—especially if it's your first project. You'll also learn how to select fabrics and trims that are appropriate to your project and skill level. Then it's on to "the scary part"—calculating yardages—which really is anything but! Although some slipcovering methods require multiple, painstaking measurements and lay-outs, my simplified approach makes use of yardage charts or a few key measurements. When you use these as basic guidelines, then allow for special features (such as certain skirt styles, matched prints, or positioned motifs), this approach can be just as accurate as those that take five or six times as long.

Why Slipcover?

The desire to slipcover may be grounded in style or economic needs, but either way the transformation can be notable. Among the most common reasons for slipcovering:

- **TO GIVE OLD FURNITURE NEW LIFE.** Worn or dated fabric doesn't have to be the death knell for structurally sound sofas and chairs. Choose a fabric that incorporates an up-to-date color or pattern to change the look of the piece—and perhaps the whole room.

- **TO CHANGE DESIGN LINES.** Restore formerly stylish furniture to cutting-edge elegance by raising a skirt, introducing decorative closures, or adding padding to cushions. Voilà! A whole new look.

- **TO IMPART SEASONAL INTEREST.** Give your summertime sitting room a fresh look with a new, lighter-handed wardrobe. It will put a different spin on the existing decor and save the existing upholstery.

- **TO SAVE MONEY.** In most cases, the cost of sewing your own slipcovers—or even having them custom-made—will be far less than that of purchasing replacement furniture or having an existing item reupholstered. Recycling structurally sound furniture also makes environmental sense.

- **TO PROMOTE CLEANING EASE.** No matter how careful you are, furniture can become soiled. Slipcovers to the rescue! Whether they are washable or dry-clean only, these easy-to-remove "stain guardians" will be less costly to clean than upholstery that requires a visit from specialists.

- **TO ENSURE DAMAGE CONTROL.** Even if a section of a slipcover is irreversibly damaged by a pet, food, or some other stain maker, you can simply remove the damaged section and replace it with leftover fabric—instead of replacing the whole cover.

PREVIOUS PAGE: *The illusion of a well-stocked library was created from four exquisite trompe l'oeil wallpapers from Brunschwig & Fils. A ladderback chair with rush seat is softened by adding a box-pleated cushion and a padded tabard back cover. Decorative chair ties and coordinating tufts keep the wool plaid stylishly in place.* LEFT: *In a library filled with real books, a camelback settee was integrated into the room with a busy allover print fabric slipcover. Bushy caterpillar fringe outlines the boxing on the single seat cushion.*

Assessing Furniture Choices

Embarking on your first slipcover project? Use the guidelines that follow to help select an appropriate piece for your first effort. Then build on the skills you acquire to take on more difficult pieces.

Beginner Dos and Don'ts

DO SELECT A PIECE OF FURNITURE WITH:

• **A RECTANGULAR, SQUARE, OR SYMMETRICAL FRAME DESIGN.** Curves can be hard to fit.

• **EASY ACCESS TO AREAS NEEDING TUCK-INS ALONG THE DECK AND ARMS.** (See Slipcover Checklist, on page 37.) This will make fitting easier and help ensure that the completed slipcover remains in place.

• **LIGHT-COLORED UPHOLSTERY WITH A UNIFORM SURFACE.** A subtly colored, smooth cushion will help you avoid show-through and unattractive bumps.

• **LIKE-NEW, REMOVABLE CUSHIONS.** The best cushion choices: intact rectangular or square. Nonremovable and curved cushions pose fitting challenges, and flattened or uneven cushions require rebuilding.

• **A LIMITED AREA TO COVER.** The larger the piece, the more work and fabric required. Shy away from the 10-foot sofa, and stick to the club or Parsons chair your first time out.

AVOID FURNITURE WITH:

• **VINYL OR LEATHER UPHOLSTERY.** Slipcover fabric will slip and slide, making pinfitting a challenge, and the completed slipcover will shift constantly.

• **OPEN OR PARTIALLY UPHOLSTERED ARMS OR A LOT OF VISIBLE WOOD.** These are difficult to work with and some simply don't lend themselves to slipcovers.

• **MOVING PARTS.** Recliners, platform rockers, and swivel chairs often won't sit still for pin-fitting, and they pose a host of construction problems.

• **BUTTONS, TUFTS, OR CHANNEL BACK.** The grooves these designs incorporate make getting a smooth back difficult, and filling in those grooves with batting or foam is a job best left to the experienced slipcoverer.

• **NUMEROUS CURVES OR BARREL SHAPES.** Curves complicate the pin-fitting process. You may want to work your way up to the wing chair.

RIGHT: *This classic English lounge chair with loose pillow back was structurally sound, and therefore an ideal piece for slipcovering. The cover was designed without a separate skirt to allow the cotton print to star and simplify the seaming. Extra fabric and time were required to achieve these results.*

Fabric Choices

The fabric you select will dictate a great deal about your slipcover project: its look; feel; life expectancy; and, perhaps most important, degree of difficulty. Sometimes it's easy to be mesmerized by a beautiful fabric—then become disillusioned two hours into the project when you realize the fabric isn't appropriate for you or your slipcover. However, if you're absolutely inspired to create a slipcover in metallic organza, let your vision carry you onward—just be ready to exercise extra patience. A good rule of thumb: Select a fabric of the highest quality you can afford that offers properties that fit with your style, experience, and timetable. When in doubt, use the "Fabric Suitability Checklist," which follows, and refer to "Fabric Options," on page 16.

Fabric Suitability Checklist

1. **PLAIN OR PRINT?** Plain fabrics with an allover, nondirectional design make the fastest and easiest slipcovers. Large prints and wide stripes will require matching for a professional look, which translates to more time and fabric and a higher level of skill.

2. **NATURAL OR SYNTHETIC?** Natural fabrics look and wear best. Cool, smooth cotton is the most popular and versatile for slipcovers because it's easy to gather and crease, wears well, and hugs furniture nicely. Luckily, it's available in an enormous array of colors and prints. Linen is another favorite, but looks best on loose, casual covers because of its high wrinkle quotient. Pure synthetics tend to be slippery and don't wear well; however, blends with no more than 40 percent synthetic fibers can work but will have a tendency to pucker at seams.

3. **IS IT APPROPRIATE TO MY SKILL LEVEL?** Size up the fabric's traits, then assess your own. For example, if you're considering a large or bold print, are you comfortable with placing and matching motifs? If the fabric is heavy, can you work with its bulk or weight? And if the fabric's right side is barely distinguishable from its wrong side, can you provide the requisite attention to detail?

4. **HOW WELL WILL IT WEAR?** Look for fabrics with high thread counts, good give and recover prop-

erties, and stain-release finishes. Tightly woven, stain-resistant fabrics make for durable covers that wear well. Loose weaves are likely to stretch out of shape, wear unevenly, and ravel.

5. WILL IT BE APPROPRIATE AS A SLIPCOVER? Is the size and scale of the fabric design appropriate? Positioning large, bold motifs in the middle of a chair back or in the center of a cushion can prove dramatic—and can be particularly appropriate on larger pieces—but can also require a lot of fabric. Will the pattern reverse effectively so both sides of the piece of furniture will appear to match? If not, you're inviting disappointment.

6. WILL ITS COLOR FADE WHEN IT'S LAUNDERED? Look for the terms "Vat Dyed" and "Vat Colors" along the fabric selvage; these mean the fabric is fade resistant.

7. IS IT OPAQUE? Lining is not generally recommended on slipcovers. If loose weave, light weight, or bleed-through calls for something underneath the slipcover, choose a more suitable fabric or consider making a muslin slipcover for use beneath the primary slipcover. Exceptions are simple slipcovers for "pull-up chairs," such as many of those in Part 3, which may be lined.

8. HOW FREQUENTLY WILL CLEANING BE REQUIRED? Color, fiber, and your usage habits will be factors. In general, light colors and dry-clean-only fibers aren't good choices for high-use areas or children's rooms, but are fine for an infrequently used room. Consider the planned cleaning method before buying and, unless the selvage indicates the fabric is preshrunk, plan to do so (see page 16, Prepare—Preshrink!, for details).

9. CAN MY SEWING MACHINE HANDLE IT? The machine you use can be as basic as they come (even straight stitch only), but it must be in good working condition to stitch through the bulk you'll encounter where slipcover seams intersect—commonly four to six layers when welting is involved. Heavy, upholstery-weight fabrics aren't recommended for slipcovers, not only because they're difficult to shape, but also because they can put your general-use sewing machine out of commission.

OPPOSITE PAGE, TOP TO BOTTOM: *Three good choices for slipcover fabrics include cotton prints; plain solid linen, lined and quilted; and woven Jacquard.* RIGHT: *Tulips dance all over this slipcover cut from beautiful cotton fabric hand-printed in Italy with more than twenty different color screens. The large repeat is artistically positioned and perfectly matched as it covers the back, seat cushion, and long dressmaker skirt.*

Prepare—Preshrink!

Unless you purchase preshrunk fabric, *preshrinking is never optional*. Preshrink your fabric according to the care method you plan to use for the completed slipcover—either dry-clean or wash it.

If you plan to wash the slipcover, first conduct this test:

1. Cut two identical test pieces from the fabric (9 inches by half the fabric width is an adequate size).

2. Wash one piece on your washer's gentle cycle in cold water. Dry it on low heat, removing it while still damp. Let it air-dry completely.

3. Compare the washed sample to the unwashed sample to check for fading, wrinkling, and shrinking. If there is an excessive amount of any of the three, dry-clean the fabric to preshrink it and plan to dry-clean the completed slipcover when it needs cleaning.

Note: Shrinkage is most likely to occur along the lengthwise grain. If the amount of shrinkage is acceptable and you plan to wash your fabric, be sure you have allowed enough fabric to compensate for shrinkage.

Also, keep these tips in mind:

• Preshrink all fabric destined to become welting (especially important if the welting may bleed), zippers, and any other kind of closure or trim. To preshrink trim, use the same cleaning method you'll use on the slipcover fabric.

Note: Zippers and washable trims can be preshrunk by dipping them in warm water and letting them drip-dry.

• Select only those trims whose care is compatible with the care of the slipcover fabric. For example, if you plan to make a washable slipcover with welting, select polyester cord for welting, rather than shrink-prone cotton cord. Likewise, save delicate trims for use on dry-clean-only slipcovers.

• When creating the slipcover from preshrunk fabric, *do not* cut the pieces larger to allow for residual shrinkage. Instead, cut as needed for a good fit. When it's time to clean the slipcover, launder as you did to preshrink the fabric and place the damp slipcover on the furniture to air-dry, fastening closures to ensure the cover stays in place.

Fabric Options

When considering fabrics for a slipcover project, keep in mind each fabric's image (elegant, casual, whimsical, etc.), cost, durability, and sewability. Then select one that matches your style, budget, usage plans, and skill level. A list of the most popular slipcover options follows.

Barkcloth: Woven drapery fabric with rough or barklike appearance.

Bedford cord: Sturdy, ribbed fabric with raised lengthwise cord; may be woven of cotton, silk, wool, or synthetic fibers.

Broadcloth: Densely textured cloth with plain or twill weave and lustrous finish; may be woven of cotton, silk, wool, or synthetic fibers.

Brocade: Rich, heavy-looking cloth with woven pattern; cotton brocade is often woven with other yarns to create silky pattern on matte background.

Calico: Plain-weave, lightweight fabric similar to percale, printed with small figures; originally all cotton, today often a blend of polyester and cotton.

Canvas: Heavy, strong, firmly woven cotton, linen, or synthetic fabric; may be soft-finished or highly sized.

Chambray: Fine-quality plain-weave fabric with linenlike finish, combining colored warp and white filling yarns; woven in solids, stripes, and checks or patterned with Jacquard designs.

Chino: Coarse cotton fabric woven of combed yarns in twill weave; usually preshrunk.

Chintz: Plain-weave cotton fabric with glazed surface in solid colors or prints; tends to be slippery and stiff, may need extra seams to achieve needed shaping.

Corduroy: Cut-pile fabric woven in either plain or twill weave with lengthwise wales, cords, or ribs of varying widths, as in pinwale and wide wale. Difficult slipcover fabric: tends to slip and shift during sewing, and matching wide wales can be problematic.

Cotton (below): Used in weaving organdy, broadcloth, poplin, and corduroy. Cotton fabrics are strong, comfortable, absorbent, and static-free. They dye well but tend to wrinkle, deteriorate from mildew, and shrink badly if untreated. Cotton is the most popular fiber for slipcover fabric.

Damask: Fabric woven on Jacquard loom to produce figured designs by combining different weave patterns; often incorporating satin-weave patterns against plain or twill background.

Denim: Strong, coarse, washable, twill-weave fabric of cotton or cotton blend, with colored warp and white filling yarns; may be solid, striped, or plaid. One of many dressmaking fabrics suitable for slipcover use.

Dobby: Fabric, such as piqué, that incorporates small geometric patterns. The patterns are woven by an attachment to a specialty loom.

Drill: Strong, twill-weave cotton fabric similar to denim. When dyed olive drab, drill is called khaki.

Duck: See Sailcloth.

Flannel: Soft plain- or twill-weave fabric with slightly napped surface on one or both sides.

Gabardine: Firm, tightly woven fabric with close diagonal twill-weave surface and flat back; may be woven of wool, cotton, or synthetic blends. Usually piece-dyed and finished with high sheen.

Khaki: Sturdy twill-weave cloth of cotton or wool; cotton or cotton-blend khaki are washable and would make easy-care casual slipcovers.

Linen: Strong, lustrous, absorbent fiber from flax plants; made into a range of items, from sheer handkerchief weights to heavy, coarse weaves. Usually imported from Ireland or Belgium. Can be a difficult slipcover fabric: Linen wrinkles, ravels, and shifts easily. Most suitable for casual, loose-fitting slipcovers.

Muslin: Any of a wide variety of plain-weave cotton fabrics ranging from sheer to heavy sheeting; can be unbleached, bleached, dyed in solid colors, or printed. May be used to make underlying slipcover when primary slipcover fabric is loosely woven, lightweight, or not opaque. Also used for making templates (see **Template,** on page 108).

Piqué: Dobby-weave fabric with raised, lengthwise cords, welts, or wales; available with a variety of plain or patterned effects.

Polished Cotton: Cotton fabric with shiny surface achieved through satin weave or waxed finish.

Poplin: Plain-weave fabric with fine rib running from selvage to selvage; similar to cotton or rayon broadcloth but with slightly heavier rib. May be woven of silk, cotton, rayon, wool, or blends.

Sailcloth: Heavy, strong, extremely durable plain-weave canvas fabric woven of cotton, linen, synthetics, or blends; woven in plain or rib weaves in various weights. Also called duck.

Silk: Continuous protein filament produced by silkworm larva as it builds a cocoon. Available in a variety of weights and weaves, from sheer chiffon to pongee, heavy tweeds, and brocades. Wrinkle resistant, exceptionally strong, excellent mildew and moth resistance. Dyes well but may bleed. Weakened by sunlight. Usually dry-cleaned. Many varieties are too slippery for slipcover use; most are expensive.

Synthetic Suede: Made of polyester microfiber and nonfibrous polyurethene, it has the look and feel of suede but is machine washable and dryable. Use polyester or cotton-covered polyester thread for sewing, rather than monofilament thread. Mono-filament will perforate the fabric and cause it to tear.

Taffeta: Silk or cotton plain-weave fabric that is smooth on both sides, crisp, and usually lustrous. May be plain; woven with fine rib; woven in checks, stripes, or plaid; printed; or woven with uneven threads. Weights vary from paper-thin to heavy. For slipcovers, choose a cotton variety of medium to heavy weight.

Terry Cloth (below): An absorbent toweling fabric woven with loop pile that projects on one or both sides of the cloth. Woven of cotton or polyester blends, it is ideal for bathroom or outdoor slipcovers.

Ticking: Tightly woven, sturdy cotton fabric; most often made in blue and off-white stripe. Formerly in common use as a mattress cover.

Twill: Fabric woven to produce diagonal ribs or lines on surface. Gabardine and denim are twill fabrics.

Velvet (below): Luxurious fabric with low, dense pile on one side; made of silk, rayon, cotton, nylon, polyester, or various blends. Difficult slipcover fabric: tends to slip and shift in sewing. The poly/cotton and cotton/rayon blends can be machine washed and tumbled dry, making them a more appropriate choice for slipcovers.

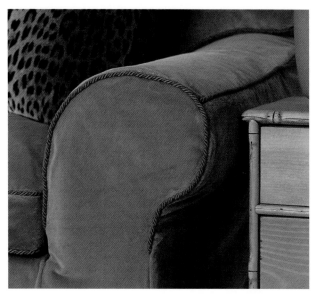

Velveteen: Soft, cut-pile cotton or synthetic on woven background with extra set of filling yarns. Difficult slipcover fabric: tends to slip and shift in sewing.

Whipcord: Twill-weave fabric, similar to gabardine, but woven using bulky yarns to create a pronounced diagonal rib on the right side.

Wool: Soft, curly fibers (fleece) with natural felting ability; taken from sheep, rabbit, goat, or llama. Difficult slipcover fabric: Fibers are weak, scratchy, and may stretch. A tightly woven wool such as classic plaids could be acceptable choices.

Sheets and More

Flat bedsheets and lightweight blankets, quilts, coverlets, and bedspreads can translate into excellent slipcover yardage. In many cases, they can help you cut down on piecing on larger furniture, they often are machine washable, and they may be considerably less expensive than fabric (this is especially true of sheets purchased at a "white" sale). Beware of different dye lots, however; colors can vary dramatically. Another option to consider is vintage fabrics that are in good condition. Old draperies, in particular, can provide great expanses of vintage fabric, but check carefully for stains and worn areas or holes.

Sheets

Buy 100 percent cotton varieties with a high thread count (200 count or higher is best), and stick with solids or small, allover prints if you're a novice. Make sure printed sheets are printed on-grain. Refer to the Sheet Yardage Conversion Chart, right, to estimate the amount of yardage you'll get from a sheet. Remember to subtract borders or decorative hems from total yardage or plan to use these features in creative ways to trim or otherwise embellish your slipcover. And if you choose a large pattern, purchase generously.

Blankets, Quilts, and Coverlets

Lightweight cotton flannel and tightly woven wool blankets, as well as lightweight quilts, will make cozy one-of-a-kind slip-

covers perfect for casual settings. Refer to the above chart to estimate the amount of yardage you'll get from each.

Bedspreads

Lightweight bedspreads—particularly delightful chenille and elegant matelassé—afford exciting slipcover fabric opportunities.

Sheet Yardage Conversion Chart

FLAT SHEET SIZE	COMMON DIMENSIONS (inches)	APPROXIMATE YARDAGE 45" width (yards)	54" width (yards)
Twin	66 × 96	4	3¼
Full	81 × 96	4¾	4
Queen	90 × 102	5¾	4¾
King	108 × 102	7	5½

Blanket, Quilt, & Coverlet Yardage Conversion Chart

BEDCOVER SIZE	COMMON DIMENSIONS (inches)	APPROXIMATE YARDAGE 45" width (yards)	54" width (yards)
Twin	66 × 90	3¾	3
	65 × 85	3¾	3
Twin/full	72 × 90	4	3½
Full	80 × 90	4½	3¾
Full/queen	85 × 95	4½	3¾
Queen	90 × 90	5	4
King	108 × 90	6	5
	105 × 95	6	5

Bedspread Yardage Conversion Chart

BEDSPREAD SIZE	COMMON DIMENSIONS (inches)	APPROXIMATE YARDAGE 45" width (yards)	54" width (yards)
Twin	78 × 108	5¼	4¼
Full	96 × 108	6½	5¼
Queen	102 × 118	7½	6
King	118 × 118	8¾	7

Determining Fabric Yardage

Once you have fabric(s) in mind, it's time to calculate how much yardage to buy. This can be done either by measuring the furniture piece and doing some basic calculations or by using a yardage estimate chart like the one on page 23.

The measurement method is the more accurate and a good idea if:

- The piece is an unusual shape.
- Your fabric is an uncommon width or has a large pattern or repeat.
- Your fabric or trim is very expensive.

The yardage estimate chart is a guideline if:

- Your piece is one of the common types covered in the chart.
- Your fabric is between 45 and 54 inches wide.
- You can afford to purchase extra yardage. (The chart suggests maximum yardages.)

The chart also serves as a handy ballpark check against your own calculations when you use the measurement method.

Note: To determine yardage for the projects featured in Part 3, refer to the individual instructions.

Measurement Method

For more precise estimates than the chart method yields, take the three basic measurements detailed in the three paragraphs that follow, then add allowances for seams, tuck-ins, and facings as directed.

Note: These measurements are for a basic slipcover. They assume you will use one fabric width per surface, except for the back and front width (Measurement A), for which you'll need to determine how many widths will be required; they *do not* account for extra yardage needed to center motifs; match repeats; or add a skirt, welting, or other embellishments. For guidelines on calculating yardage for these details, see Additional Calculations, later in this section. To help ensure accuracy, enter your measurements on a chart like the one opposite.

- **MEASUREMENT A (BACK AND FRONT).** With the cushion(s) removed, measure up from the lower edge of the chair or sofa back, up over the top, along the seat platform, and down to the front lower edge. To this measurement, add a 12-inch tuck-in allowance, 2 inches for each seam you crossed on the existing chair (except those you plan to omit on the slipcover), and a 4-inch allowance if you plan to attach a skirt or an 11-inch facing allowance if you do not plan to attach a skirt. Multiply this amount by the number of fabric widths required to cover the total width of the piece.

- **MEASUREMENT B (ARMS AND SIDES).** Measure from the lower edge of the chair or sofa side, up over the arm, and down the arm to the seat. To this measurement, add a 6-inch tuck-in allowance, 2 inches for each seam you crossed on the existing chair (except those you plan to omit on the slipcover), and a 2-inch allowance

Measurement Method Fill-in Chart

MEASUREMENT/ALLOWANCE					IN INCHES
Measurement A ____ × ____ (no. of sections or fabric widths)				=	
Measurement B ____ × _2_ (no. of arms)				=	
Measurement C ____ × ____ (no. of cushions)				=	
Pattern repeat allowance				=	
Welting allowance				=	
Skirt allowance				=	
Additional allowances[1]				=	
			Total inches		
		Divided by 36 for total yards			

[1]Such as for large-pattern placement or arm protectors, pillows, and other accents.

if you plan to attach a skirt or 5½-inch allowance if you do not plan to attach a skirt. Multiply this amount by 2 to determine the total required for the two arms.

• **MEASUREMENT C (CUSHIONS).** Measure around the cushion, front to back. To this measurement, add 2 inches for each seam you crossed. Multiply this amount by the number of cushions of this size and shape. Repeat to measure any cushions of another shape, and add together all cushion measurements.

Additional Calculations

Yardage to accommodate skirts, pattern repeats, and print placement must be determined separately, then added to the total indicated by the basic calculations.

• **SKIRTS.** Yardage will depend on the style chosen, but all skirt calculations require two measurements: the skirt length and the skirt width. Use the following formulas to determine the dimensions for various skirt styles; translate the dimensions into fabric widths; and round up to the next whole cut width, unless you plan to railroad the skirt (see **Railroading,** on page 107). For more details on skirt selection and planning, see "Skirts," on page 56, or specific project instructions in Part 3.

1. Determine the desired finished skirt length (the distance from the floor to the seamline where the skirt and slipcover meet).

For an unlined skirt, add a hem allowance (1 inch to 4 inches).

For a lined skirt, like the basic slipcover in Part 2, add ½ inch for a seam allowance and 1 inch to 3 inches for a hem allowance; for the lining, add a ½-inch seam allowance, and subtract the amount of the hem allowance used for the face fabric.

2. Determine the desired finished skirt width (the measurement around the chair at the skirtline), and add 1 inch for finishing the ends and 1 inch for each piecing seam.

For a gathered skirt, multiply by 2 to 3, depending on the fullness desired.

For a tailored skirt with pleats or gathers at the corners only, add 12 to 20 inches plus seam allowances for each full pleat or gathered area.

For a box-pleated skirt, multiply by 3¾.

For any pieced skirt, add 24 inches for hiding seams and 24 inches minimum for matching a pattern.

To determine the skirt lining width for any skirt style listed, use the same formula used for the face fabric.

- **PATTERN REPEATS.** If the fabric repeat is 3 to 12 inches, add ¾ yard for a chair, 1 yard for a love seat, and 1½ yards for a sofa; if the repeat is more than 12 inches, double these additions.

- **PATTERN PLACEMENT.** If your fabric has large motifs, you'll need to plan how those motifs will be placed on the piece (see Perfect Placement, below right), and add an extra repeat for each section, front and back, that will require special placement.

- **SELF-WELTING.** If you plan to make your own welting, determine the extra yardage required by referring to the Slipcover Yardage Estimate Chart, facing page.

- **DAMAGE INSURANCE.** Consider buying extra yardage to have on hand in the event of damage to the finished slipcover. A good rule of thumb is to allow ½ yard for a chair or 1 yard for a sofa.

Matching Motifs

When using boldly patterned fabrics, try to match motifs whenever possible. The most crucial matches: where sections are joined to create sufficient width (such as along the front or back of a sofa), where a cushion boxing strip joins the cushion top, and where a tailored skirt joins the slipcover. When using fabrics that require matching, be sure to allow extra fabric as noted with each yardage calculation method.

Perfect Placement

Fabrics with large, dominant motifs can make stunning slipcovers but will require extra yardage, careful planning, and a solid understanding of the slipcovering process. It's best for beginners to avoid using large prints until they've completed one or two projects successfully.

To use a fabric with a large design, plan your motif placement when you are calculating yardage requirements. Large designs, stripes, and plaids should be centered on all front and back sections, the side of each arm, and on each cushion. On the inside back of the chair or sofa, center the motif then move it a little more than halfway up from the center point. Measure with the cushion in place so the motif will be properly positioned on the completed piece. Avoid placing large motifs on fronts of arms, where they can look like headlights and detract from the overall piece.

To determine how much extra fabric you will need, add an extra repeat for every section that requires centering; the exact amount will differ according to the length of the repeat. For details on working with large-print fabrics, see Patterned Slipcover, on page 72.

Slipcover Yardage Estimate Chart

Yards of 45"- to 54"-Wide Plain[1] Fabric

FURNITURE TYPE	NUMBER OF CUSHIONS[2]	WITHOUT SKIRT	WITH TAILORED SKIRT (optional lining)	WITH OTHER SKIRT (optional lining)	ADDED YARDAGE FOR SELF-WELTING
Arm chair, club or lounge chair	1	5¾	6¾ (1)	8½ (2¾)	1
Wing chair, small	1	6	8 (1)	9 (2½)	1
Wing chair, large	1	7	9 (1)	10 (2¾)	1
Sofa (6' to 7')	2	16¼	18 (1¾)	21¼ (5)	1¾
Sofa (6' to 7')	3	17	18¾ (1¾)	22 (5)	1¾
Sofa (7' to 8')	3	19	21 (2½)	25 (6)	2
Love seat	2	12	13¼ (1¼)	15½ (3½)	1½
Sofa bed (to 84" wide)	2	16¼	19½ (3¼)	21¼ (5)	1¾
Sofa bed (to 84" wide)	3	17	18¾ (1¾)	22 (5)	1¾
Ottoman	1	1½	2½	4½	¾
Extra cushions (each)	—	1½	1½	1½	¼
Pillows[3] (per pair, up to 16")	—	1	1	1	¼
Pillows[3] (per pair, up to 22")	—	1½	1½	1½	½

[1] Allow extra yardage for fabrics that must be matched: If the fabric repeat is 3 to 12 inches, add ¾ yard for a chair, 1 yard for a love seat, and 1½ yards for a sofa; if the repeat is more than 12 inches, double these additions. On any project, also consider adding extra yardage for insurance against later damage: ½ yard for a chair, 1 yard for a sofa.

[2] If your piece has more cushions than noted, add yardage as noted in the Extra Cushions line of the chart.

[3] Large pillows will require more yardage; in some cases, remnants from the slipcover will be large enough for use as pillow tops and backs.

Trim Options

ABOVE: *Decorative cord with lip and a scalloped-bottom band trim define this Martha Washington chair cover that fits almost as tightly as the upholstery underneath. The faced "no-skirt" finish is described in detail on page 60.*

Trims and embellishments are often the defining and unifying touches that, when well chosen, elevate a slipcover from ordinary to exceptional. But be forewarned: Trims run the gamut in price. Some can cost as much as the slipcover, yet yield a one-of-a-kind effect that justifies the expense. However, some can be created from inexpensive matierals—ribbon, rickrack, bias fabric, etc.—so don't despair if your budget is tight. Just plan ahead and be creative in your search.

Band trim (shown at right, top and middle): Any of a wide variety of woven, embroidered, beaded, sequined, fringed, or braided ribbon or fabric finished along both edges; may be used to embellish slipcover cushions, skirts, or openings.

Bias binding (below): Prepackaged or custom-made fabric strips, usually cut on the bias; may be used as slipcover casing, facing, or embellishment. See **Binding,** on page 104.

Braid: Trim with three or more component strands plaited to form regular diagonal pattern along length; may be used to embellish slipcover cushions, skirts, or openings.

• Middy braid: Narrow flat braid made in several widths; may be used in single or multiple rows to trim slipcover hems and edges.

Chair tie (above): Cord, often with a tassel at each end, tacked to seat cushion and used to attach cushion to chair seat. May also be used as decorative detailing elsewhere on the slipcover.

Cording: See **Welting**, on page 28; may also refer to filler cord inside welting.

Cordless welting: Welting without cording filler for use when flatter trim is desired.

Cord with lip (shown with band trim, above right): Elegant twisted cord attached to braid lip for easy insertion in slipcover seams; available in cotton, wool, rayon, or silk and in solid-color and multicolor varieties. Also called cord-edge. *Note:* Choose cord diameter not greater than ¼ inch to avoid problems in sewing close enough to the cord to conceal the lip. For instructions on applying cord with lip, see Trim In-Seam Application and Trim Estimate Chart, both on page 29.

Eyelet: Lightweight fabric trim characterized by small cutout areas surrounded by decorative stitching. May be used as an element in flat or ruffled edging, galloon, flounce, or beading.

Flounce: Gathered trim, often in eyelet or lace, usually 14 inches deep; ideal for gathered skirts on feminine slipcovers.

Fringe (below): Decorative trim constructed of loose hanging strands of thread or yarn knotted and fastened to a band, or header; usually made of rayon,

silk, or polyester. May be inserted in slipcover seams singly or combined to add bulk or to customize color combinations. Styles include

- Ball fringe: Cut yarn ends fastened together to form ball, then hung from header by loop; may be used as purchased or combined to form lush decorative detail. Also called pom decor.
- Brush fringe (page 25): Lengths of cut yarn fastened together along one edge to create soft, thick brushed edge; offered in variety of lengths and thicknesses. Also called moss fringe.
- Bullion fringe (below): Tightly twisted yarn attached to header, creating spiraling, or rope, effect.
- Caterpillar fringe: Similar to brush fringe, but much fuller; cut yarns form half circle, resembling a caterpillar.
- Chainette fringe: Shimmering, cascading fringe.
- Loop fringe: Similar to brush fringe, but with ends left uncut (looped).
- Swag fringe: Scalloped fringe; often made of tubular rayon or silk cords attached to header. Also called rattail fringe.
- Tassel fringe: Tufts of cut yarn ends fastened together to form tassel; dangles from band or header.

Frog: Decorative fastener usually made of braid fashioned in an ornamental design with a loop on one side and a thick knot or button on the other; may be used as closure on slipcovers.

Galloon: Decorative braid, lace, or trim scalloped on both edges; may be used to trim slipcover hems and edges.

Gimp: Narrow, flat ornamental trim often made with loop or decorative scroll design; may be used to trim slipcover hems and edges.

Grommet (below): Metallic eyelet used to finish and stabilize fabric holes; may be used for lace-up slipcover closures.

Passementerie: Term for a wide range of trims: braid, gimp, fringe, tassels, etc.

Pinking: Zigzag edge made using special shears. A pinked edge sometimes appears along one long edge of a felt strip inserted along a seamline in expensive leather or fur furnishings; pinking may also appear in simulated suede, faux fur, or fur-print items to create an expensive-looking style. For instructions on creating and applying a pinked edging, see Butterfly Chair Cover, on page 92.

Piping: See Welting.

Ribbon: Woven trim with cord finish or simple selvage along both edges; available in a wide range of fibers—such as cotton, polyester, rayon, or silk—and many weaves and widths beginning at $\frac{1}{16}$ inch. May be used as edging and ornamentation on a wide variety of slipcovers. For example, consider using $1\frac{1}{2}$-inch-wide grosgrain ribbon for making welting (see Parsons Chair, on page 80). Or use your sewing machine's pleater attachment to pleat $\frac{7}{8}$-inch-wide double-faced satin ribbon, then insert it in focal seams. Ribbon styles include

• Grosgrain ribbon (below): Closely woven, corded, narrow trim; available in a wide range of solids as well as woven stripes and prints.

• Jacquard ribbon: Narrow trim woven on Jacquard loom, which is capable of creating intricate designs; typical designs include multicolor florals, reversible patterns, and scroll or paisley motifs with metallic accents.

• Picot-edge ribbon: Narrow trim with small thread loops along edges, sometimes with knots or stitches added.

Rickrack: Readily available zigzag-shaped woven trim available in wide range of colors; may be applied along slipcover seamlines—singularly or two colors braided together—to create whimsical, undulating effect.

Ruched cord: Light- to mediumweight fabric tube sewn over cord like welting, but with fabric cut 2 to $2\frac{1}{2}$ times the desired finished length and gathered to create fullness; may be used wherever welting is used.

Ruffling: Fabric strips cut on bias (or with the grain, to conserve fabric), folded in half lengthwise, and gathered along cut edges; may be used to add soft touch to slipcover skirts. For instructions on different methods for gathering ruffling, see **Gathering,** on page 105.

Tassel: Pendant ornament consisting of a tuft of loosely hanging threads or cord; may be used at slipcover cushion or skirt corners. See Making Your Own Tassel Ties, on page 28.

Tieback: Decorative cord, often with tassel ornament, designed for holding back drapery panel; may be used as tie for seat cushion or to decorate back of chair slipcover.

Tufts (below): A cluster of threads drawn tightly through cushions to secure the stuffing and add decorative detail.

Welting: Traditional seam-line trim. Also called piping or cording. May be purchased or made by wrapping soft cotton cord with fabric bias strips cut from slipcover fabric or from contrasting or coordinating fabric. *Self-welting* (below), refers to welting made of the same fabric as the slipcover. For instructions on creating and applying welting, see **Welting,** on page 108.

Determining Trim Yardage

Like fabric yardage, trim yardage can be estimated using a chart (see Trim Estimate Chart, on facing page) or calculated precisely by measuring the piece to be slipcovered. To get an accurate calculation, measure all the seams to be trimmed, add these measurements together, and add an additional yard. Keep in mind that, when slipcovering, the number and placement of slipcover seams will be different from those on the original upholstered piece, so be clear about your plan before you purchase—or add a couple extra yards of trim to allow for surprises.

Making Your Own Tassel Ties

Tassels add elegance to cushion or skirt corners or formal slipcovers. To save a bundle on purchased tassels, learn how to create these classic embellishments from embroidery floss.

1. To make a 27-inch chair tie with tassel ends approximately 3 inches long, cut a piece of cardboard 4 inches long and at least 4 inches wide. (Adjust the length of the cardboard for longer or shorter tassels.) Purchase 6-strand embroidery floss in the desired color or colors. Allow 13 skeins for each chair tie with 2 tassels.

2. Wrap the floss around the cardboard lengthwise 144 times with the 2 cut ends at the bottom edge. The number of times you wrap the cardboard will determine the fullness of the finished tassel. Slip a 6-inch piece of strong thread under the floss at the top of the cardboard and tie ends of thread securely to draw the strands together. Cut the floss at the bottom of the cardboard. Make 2 tassels for each tie.

3. To make the tie-on cords, cut 24 pieces of floss, each 36 inches long. Lay the strands together and knot them 3 inches from one end. Braid the strands for 27 inches and tie another knot, leaving the ends unbraided.

4. Tie the unbraided ends of the cord around the tassel, covering the thread you used to secure the bundle. Fold the tassel lengths in half over the knot.

5. To make the tassel head, wrap three 6-strand pieces of floss securely around the tassel about ¾ inch down from the top, and knot the ends. Thread the floss ends into a large-eyed needle and "weave" the ends inside the tassel.

6. Shake out the tassel to free the strands and trim the bottom ends to even the length.

Trim In-Seam Application

Fringe and cord with lip are both well suited to being caught in seams, creating a polished, sophisticated finish.

To insert fringe in a seam

1. Leave intact any temporary chain stitching holding the fringe together. If the fringe doesn't have any chain stitching, carefully secure the fringe with masking or transparent tape (test first to be sure the tape won't harm the fringe) to keep it from moving about and getting caught in the seam.

2. Position the fringe heading completely within the seam allowance so none of it will show on the completed treatment; baste the fringe heading in place just above the lower edge of the heading.

3. During the construction of the window treatment, plan your stitching so it falls within the fringe, just below the lower edge of the heading.

4. Remove chain stitching, any tape, and basted stitches to complete.

To insert cord with lip in a seam

1. Position the lip completely within the seam allowance so none of it will show on the completed treatment; using a zipper foot, baste the lip in place just above its lower edge.

2. During the construction of the window treatment, plan your stitching so it falls at the point where the cord joins the lip. Remove the basted stitches.

Trim Estimate Chart

FURNITURE TYPE	NUMBER OF CUSHIONS	CORD FOR WELTING OR DECORATIVE TRIM (yards)	YARDAGE TO COVER CORD FOR WELTING	SKIRT HEM EMBELLISHMENT	
				TAILORED (yards)	OTHER (yards)
Arm chair, club or lounge chair	1	18	1	5	10–12
Wing chair, small	1	15	1	4	9–11
Wing chair, large	1	18	1	5	10–12
Sofa (6' to 7')	2	36	$1\frac{3}{4}$	7	12–16
	3	41	$1\frac{7}{8}$	7	12–16
Sofa (7' to 8')	3	45	2	8	13–18
Love seat	2	24	$1\frac{1}{2}$	6	10–15
Ottoman		6–9	$\frac{1}{2}$	3–4	5–8
Extra cushions (each)		5	$\frac{1}{4}$		
Pillow (16")		$1\frac{3}{4}$	$\frac{1}{4}$		
(22")		$2\frac{1}{2}$	$\frac{1}{4}$		

Note: This chart is a guide to help in planning your slipcover design; before purchasing trim, measure your specific piece of furniture.

Creating Slipcovers

It's time to have some fun! The techniques and instructions in this section will guide you step-by-step through the process of creating a slipcover for a basic square-back chair with a cushion, curved arms, straight skirt, and traditional welting of solid-color fabric. This simple, straightforward project is the basic template for slipcovering any upholstered piece; more elaborate projects can be created by adding more, or more complex, elements. For details about creating a slipcover for a sofa, love seat, or sofa bed, see Slipcovering Wide Furniture, on page 41. To apply the concepts to ottomans, see Slipcovering Ottomans, on page 42.

Review:
- [ ] Review:
    Part 1 - Before You Begin.
    Slipcover Tools (p. 100).
    Basic Slipcover Materials (p.101).
- [ ] Buy supplies.
- [ ] Familiarize yourself with terms and techniques in Part 4.
- [ ] Read Part 2 to get a clear overview of how slipcover will be constructed.
- [ ] Cut the fabric!

PREVIOUS PAGE: *A dramatic, verdant green fern print on practical cotton poplin fabricates streamlined covers for upholstered Parsons chairs.* LEFT: *Cushy, casual, and oh so comfortable suede cloth covers a lounge chair with loose pillow back and T-cushion. The printed stripe pattern was cut to create a band trim to edge the skirt bottom together with self-bias welting. Keep your reading materials within easy reach with a generous pocket attached to the slipcover's outside arm. Elastic in a casing controls the pocket top but allows easy storage for magazines and papers.* OPPOSITE: *Tiger skin-patterned needlepoint fabric boldly covers a basic ottoman. Eliminate boxing seams and create fit by mitering the fabric. To help keep the slipcover tucked under the top cushion, tie a length of twill tape tightly in the crevice. Outrageous loop fringe adds whimsy to a traditional wing chair slipcover cut from tough cotton canvas. Because the header on the fringe is thick, be sure to allow generous allowances at the seams to accommodate the extra bulk.* RIGHT: *Slipcovering chairs of different styles with the same fabric is an easy way to unify your design scheme.*

LEFT: *Seat cushions can have a softer look with bias ruffles and perky bows or can be tailored with a knife edge and contrasting cord on lip. Some chairs are too special to hide under a full slipcover. Tie-on covers expose the carved chair frame and caning back while adding the comfort of seat and back cushions. If you sew covered buttons to both sides of seat pads, you can attach them to the chair with coordinating grosgrain ribbon that is slit to fit over the button, then threaded through the caning and tied in bows to secure.* RIGHT: *Slipcovering just two of the Queen Anne chairs at this table immediately created special host and hostess chairs and introduced fabric to the expanse of wood. Have fun designing your slipcovers. Consider many different fabric options. Choose unusual trimming such as this double-face satin ribbon that we pleated to replace the expected welting, and finish the cover with elegant pearl buttons that not only act as closures, but add shimmer and detailing to the chair back.*

Slipcover Basics

The first step in *creating* an effective slipcover is *visualizing* an effective slipcover. Sketch your planned project or take a photo of the existing piece and sketch over it with markers, grease pencils, or even crayons to simulate the changes you will make. As you visualize, keep in mind the following:

• The placement and number of seams need not follow the upholstery seams. However, all seams must be symmetrical from one side of the furniture piece to the other (unless the piece is asymmetrical, as in the case of a one-arm chair). A good rule of thumb for slipcover seam placement: Simplify wherever possible, especially at the top, side and back panels, and front arm panels. For example, if the chair has a square back and square arms, you will need separate top, back, and back arm panels; however, if a chair has a rounded back and rounded arms, you can cover the top, back, and back arm areas with one panel. Likewise, you can often create side and back panels as one to avoid unnecessary seams. If there isn't a top arm panel (such as on rounded arms), you must create a seam between

ABOVE: *A jumbo gingham-checked linen was chosen to transform this dated pink chair. While studying ideas, we decided to cut the slipcover on the bias in order to create an imaginative sawtooth hem.*

The Slipcovering Process

The slipcovering method presented here will guide you through four basic steps:

1. Blocking—cutting individual fabric sections to correspond to each section of the chair or sofa, allowing enough extra fabric to pin the seams and to tuck fabric into crevices.

2. Pin-fitting—pinning the sections together on the sofa or chair to determine the exact placement of the seams.

3. Trimming—cutting off excess fabric to within ½ inch of the intended seam and marking seamlines.

4. Sewing—repinning and stitching the pin-fitted seams, with or without welting or other seam trim.

the inside and outside arms, as shown in the illustration on page 38.

• Large motifs must be centered on the sections of the furniture piece. Refer to Perfect Placement, on page 22, for more details.

• Plaids must be matched and stripes aligned. For details on matching, refer to the general instructions in Matching Motifs, on page 22, and Patterned Slipcover, on page 72.

• **Railroading** the fabric (see page 107) is not recommended because the stretch and recover capabilities are affected when the fabric direction is changed.

• A slipcover can be made with one of several types of skirts or with no skirt. For details on skirt choices, see "Skirts," on page 56.

• Closure options abound. Although this basic slipcover features the most common closure—a zipper —consider other choices that are fashionable and functional. See "Closures," on page 61.

• Self-welting will blend into the slipcover and therefore call less attention to the seams than will contrasting trims, which tend to frame the piece. An overview of trim choices can be found on pages 24–28.

• Not every seam must be trimmed, especially if you use a bulky trim like brush fringe. Carefully visualize where your trim will be placed and review the slipcovers throughout this book. *Note:* If you eliminate trim at some seams, be sure to adjust total trim yardage accordingly.

Slipcover Checklist

Have you forgotten anything? As you block and pin-fit your slipcover, use the quick-reference list that follows to keep track of your progress. Work in the order shown in the list. The letters in the list refer to the areas labeled in the accompanying illustration.

❑ Inside back (A)

❑ Top boxing (B)

❑ Inside arm (C)— cut two

❑ Outside arm (D) —cut two

❑ Outside back (E)

❑ Front apron (F)

❑ Deck (G)

❑ Front arm panel (H)—cut two

❑ Shoulder (I)—cut two

❑ Cushion top and bottom (J)

❑ Cushion boxing (K)

❑ Skirt (L)

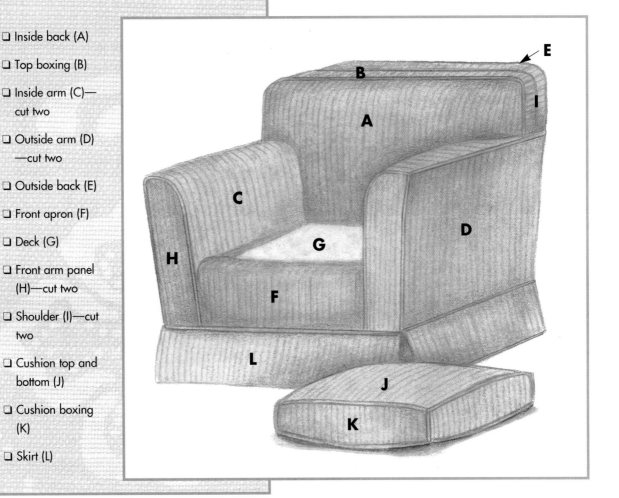

Blocking

The following points are important to keep in mind as you proceed through the blocking process. They *will not be repeated* with each step of "Blocking: Specifics," on page 40.

Blocking: General Guidelines

• Removable markings on the chair will help you know where to begin and end sections as you block your slipcover. First, decide on the depth of the skirt, if the cover will have one. Using chalk and a ruler, mark around the four sides of the chair at the desired skirt height. Next, mark the placement of the seam that will join the inner and outer arm panels. This seam may follow the seam on the upholstery or, on curved or rolled arms without a seam, the slipcover seam should fall at the thickest part of the arm. To find the exact location of that seam, place a yardstick upright against the outside arm and mark the point where the stick touches the arm. Mark this point at the front and back of the arm; use a yardstick to draw a straight line between these two points (see the dotted line in the illustration below).

• To fit well and stay in place, a basic slipcover must be tucked in along the chair deck back and side

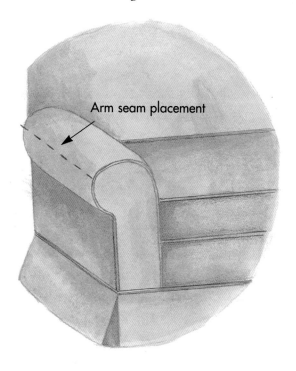

Arm seam placement

edges, where the deck meets the chair back and arms. In addition, your chair may allow tuck-ins along the inner arms, where they meet the chair back. Always check the furniture piece for the availability and depth of tuck-in areas. To check the tuck-in depth, insert a ruler into the crevice; in most cases, 4 inches is an ample tuck-in.

• A slipcover is easier to make if you can block it and pin-fit it with the right side of the fabric against the existing upholstery. (The fabric needs to be seam side out for sewing so, if you can block the sections right side down, you avoid having to turn and repin them before joining the pieces.) On most patterned fabric, the design shows through to the wrong side clearly enough for centering and matching. However, if you're working with a print that does not show through well or you simply want to view your slipcover's progress more clearly, working with the fabric right side out is perfectly acceptable. Just remember that you will need to repin the seams so the fabrics are right sides together before you sew.

• To keep large amounts of fabric manageable, work with the fabric straight from the roll or bolt, unrolling only slightly more fabric than you need as you block each section, and allowing the remainder to rest on the floor.

• If you've chosen a fabric without an obvious right and wrong side, mark the wrong side with chalk along the full length of the goods. This will save time and prevent mistakes as you place the fabric on the furniture.

• On all vertical fabric panels, position the fabric with the lengthwise grain running straight up and down from the floor. On the deck, cushion(s), and the top back panels, position the fabric with the lengthwise grain running from front to back.

• Trim off all selvages; they may pucker or distort the shape of the fabric if used as seam allowances.

• If you plan to create welting from the same fabric as the slipcover, be sure to set aside enough fabric for this before you begin blocking the slipcover.

• If you're concerned about having enough yardage, cut out the longest and widest panels first—

inside back, cushion top and bottom, inside and out-side arms—and *cut generously*. If you make a mistake, these panels can be recut for use as smaller sections. Also, the deck and back panels can be pieced if nec-essary; the pattern doesn't have to match if fabric sup-ply is tight and the furniture will be against a wall.

• During blocking and cutting, use T-pins to secure the fabric as needed. Begin by pinning each fabric section at the chair section center point to sta-bilize the section and help keep the fabric on grain.

• To cut each fabric panel, smooth the fabric yardage outward from the center, then upward and downward over the section; do not stretch or pull the fabric. **Unless otherwise noted, allow 2 inches for seam allowance along any edge where the panel will join another panel in an exposed seam or 4 inches for tuck-in allowance along any edge**

Choose a simple shape for your first slipcovering project. The square lines, symmetrical shape, and tight back make our basic chair an appropriate beginner's piece.

where the panel will tuck into a furniture crevice. If your chair has a spring-edge deck that springs up and down at the front edge, leave a greater tuck-in allowance at the front corners to keep the slipcover seam from ripping when you sit down. Also follow any special instructions given for each panel in "Blocking: Specifics," the next section.

• It's best to leave the blocked pieces pinned to the upholstery as you work, even if you have to pin some edges up out of the way when blocking other sec-tions. If you must remove them, first carefully chalk-mark the panel position clearly (such as *IB* for *inside back*). Also, use a *T* or an *F* to indicate the top or front.

• After you have gained experience cutting slipcovers, you may save time by blocking two panels at once for mirror-image areas, such as inside arms, outside arms, and front arm panels. This is called **double-cutting** (see page 105).

Blocking: Specifics

Although the order of the steps detailed in this section is flexible, I find the progression outlined below works well. As you read the steps that follow, you'll find that each section of the chair is defined and keyed to the chair illustration on page 37. Then the text presents any special instructions for blocking that section. You will be adding a 2-inch seam allowance (unless otherwise noted) at every edge where fabric will be joined.

1. INSIDE BACK (A). The inside chair back from the top edge to the top of the deck.

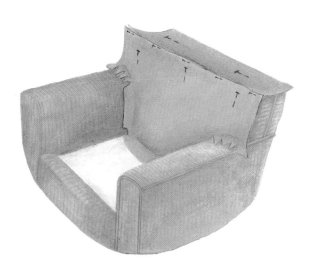

2. TOP BOXING (B). The top of the chair back (only on square-back furniture). Allow 3 inches all around for minor adjustments.

3. INSIDE ARM (C). The area along the inside arm, up over the top of the arm, to the outside arm seamline. Allow for a tuck-in at the crevice between the inside arm and the deck and, if your chair will accommodate it, a tuck-in at the meeting of inside arm and back. Cut one inside arm for each side. To determine the seam position, refer to the illustration on page 38.

4. OUTSIDE ARM (D). Along the outside of the arm, the area beginning at a seamline and continuing along the length of the arm to the skirtline. Don't forget to allow 2 inches of fabric below the marked skirtline. Cut one outside arm for each side.

5. OUTSIDE BACK (E). The area covering the entire back of the chair down to the skirtline. Allow 2 inches of fabric below the marked skirtline. You will need to consider your closure choice at this time. The basic slipcover created in this part features a corner zipper closure. For details on how to block, pin, and sew this and other closures, see "Closures," on page 61.

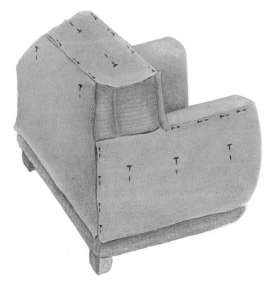

Slipcovering Wide Furniture

The same techniques used to slipcover a basic chair can also be used to create slipcovers for more expansive furniture like sofas, love seats, and sofa beds. Use these tips and techniques as needed to modify the instructions throughout Part 2:

- On sofas with vertical upholstery welting, duplicate those seams on the inside back with welting. On the outside back and the deck, use just two fabric widths with a seam in the center. On the deck, you can railroad the fabric if needed (see **Railroading,** on page 107).

- If you're using a distinctly patterned fabric, it is imperative that you cut each inside back section so the identical pattern appears in each section. Also, the pattern on each seat cushion must align with its corresponding section on the inside back, as well as with the back cushions (if there are any). You'll need two or three fabric widths each for the inside and outside backs, the front apron, and the deck. For more details on matching, refer to the instructions for the Patterned Slipcover, on page 72.

- On sofas with crevices between the sections, seam and welt without tuck-ins.

- Closure placement on sofas is usually down one of the interior seams on the back, for ease of dressing.

- If you're planning a kick-pleated skirt, plan a pleat at each front seam.

- Cut the panels for each cushion cover separately—no two are the same.

6. FRONT APRON (F). The area extending across the width of the chair front, from the deck down to the skirtline.

7. DECK (G). The area extending from the upper edge of the front apron to the chair back. Allow for tuck-ins along the sides and back. *Note:* Before cutting out the deck, outside back and arm, and back panels, be sure you have enough fabric remaining to cut the skirt as desired. If you are short on fabric sub-stitute a second fabric for the deck, such as muslin. For details on cutting and creating the straight skirt used on the basic slipcover in this part, or for other skirt options, refer to "Skirts," on page 56.

8. FRONT ARM (H). The area at the front of the arm extending from the upper arm down to the front apron. From remaining smaller pieces, cut one front arm for each side. Allow as much as 4 inches all around for adjusting placement.

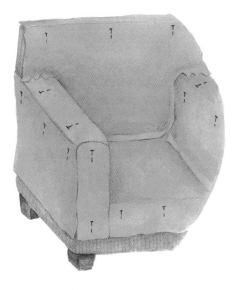

9. SHOULDER (I). Also called the side back, the depth of the seat back, extending from the arm upward to the top back. From remaining smaller pieces, cut one shoulder for each side. Allow as much as 4 inches all around for adjusting placement.

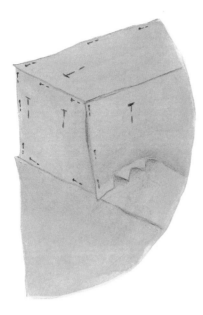

10. CUSHION COVER (TOP AND BOTTOM [J] AND BOXING [K]). The area on the top and bottom of the cushion and the band around the cushion depth that includes a zipper for access to the cushion. For the cushion cover top and bottom, measure the cushion top length and width, and cut two identical pieces slightly larger than those measurements, with the lengthwise grain running from the cushion back to front. If you are working with a large motif, cut the cushion top after the inside back to ensure perfect

Slipcovering Ottomans

Ottomans, hassocks, and footstools are blocked and pin-fitted using the same procedure used for the basic chair slipcover. Use these guidelines to modify those instructions:

• If the ottoman is a basic rectangle, you can cut the pieces based on measurements rather than blocking on the piece of furniture.

• Because an ottoman is seen from all sides, the seams should fall at the corners. On ottomans with skirts, be sure to hide the skirt seams in pleats or gathers.

• No closure is required for ottomans—the cover is slipped over the top.

• For ottomans that have the appearance of a loose pillow top, ignore the crevice between the pillow and base. Instead, create a welted seam at that level to create a visual separation of top and skirt.

• If an ottoman is to match a chair covered in a print fabric, block the fabric on the ottoman to match or complement the fabric placement on the chair.

• Ottomans can have the same skirt options, or the faced no-skirt option, as other furniture. If mated to a chair, an ottoman should have the same skirt as the accompanying piece.

placement (see Patterned Slipcover, on page 72). To create the cushion boxing, cut one strip long enough to cover the back of the cushion plus 3½ inches to extend around each side. This is where the zipper will later be installed. The remaining boxing strip extends across the cushion front and joins the back boxing on the sides of the seat. To complete the zipper strip, unpin the back boxing strip and use it as a pattern to cut a second zipper strip. Fold one strip in half lengthwise and press. *Note:* You may need to piece the long cushion boxing band.

11. SKIRT (L). The treatment at the lower edge of the slipcover. For details on cutting and creating the kick-pleat skirt used on the basic slipcover, see "Creating and Attaching the Skirt," on page 48. For alternatives refer to "Skirts," on page 56.

Pin-Fitting

Accurate pin-fitting is the key to a proper fit, so practice patience. Take your time and repin when necessary. *Note:* The steps in pin-fitting should occur in the same sequence as the steps in blocking. For more guidance on pin-fitting, refer to the illustrations accompanying "Blocking: Specifics," on pages 40–42.

Pin-Fitting: General Guidelines

The following points are important to keep in mind as you proceed through the pin-fitting process. They *will not be repeated* with each step of "Pin-Fitting: Specifics."

• Although T-pins are ideal for the blocking process, dressmaker's pins or long quilter's pins are best for pin-fitting.

• On all slipcover panels, pin the panel to the upholstery at the center point (if you left the panels in place after blocking, this will be done already). Then smooth the fabric toward the sides and corners, pinning in lines from the center to the edges and positioning pins closer together as you near the perimeter.

• When the panel is anchored in position, pin each seam exactly where you want the stitching lines unless otherwise noted. Position the pins approximately 1 inch apart, being careful not to pin the upholstery.

• Finish pinning one seam before you proceed to the next. Pin all seams that you can for each section.

• Where possible, leave final seam allowance trimming until the end of the pin-fitting process. You can cut away some of the excess fabric as you go, but try to leave at least 1 inch for final adjustments. When pin-fitting is complete, trim all seam allowances to ½ inch.

• Where necessary on panels with curves or angles, use **clipping** (see page 104) for outward curves or **notching** (see page 106) for inward curves. This will permit seam allowances to fit into the next section.

• Wherever tuck-in edges join, flare the seam diagonally outward to leave ½-inch seam allowances at the corner.

• Control slipcover fullness at furniture corners and curved areas with **gathers, darts,** or **miters.** Or if the fullness is minor, use **easing** when you sew the seam. (The boldface terms are explained in Part 4.)

• Compete all mirror-image panels in pairs—first one side, then the other—before moving on to the next section.

Pin-Fitting: Specifics

Again, although the order of the steps detailed in this section is flexible, I find the progression used for blocking works well. *As you work, keep in mind all the tips and techniques detailed in the previous section and follow any additional instructions noted for each chair section.*

1. INSIDE BACK (A). Where the inside back panel meets the chair arm, push the fabric gently toward the crevice. To get a smooth fit, clip the seam allowance once at the point where the inside back begins to shape outward along the arm, then make additional clips on each side of the first until you get a smooth fit.

2. TOP BOXING (B). Center the top boxing panel on the chair. Pin it to the inside back panel, making sure the seamline aligns precisely along the edge and doesn't roll toward the top.

3. INSIDE ARM (C). Remember that you need tuck-in allowances between the inside arm and inside back panels and between the inside arm and deck panels. Also allow at least 2 inches beyond the seamline where the inside and outside arm panels will join. Carefully slit the curved areas of the inside arm panel exactly as you did the inside back panel in the same area. In the slit area, pin the inside arm panel as closely as possible to the arm crevice; place the pins perpendicular to the future seam.

4. OUTSIDE ARM (D). Reposition the outside arm panel as needed to keep it perpendicular to the floor, even if the upholstery is not. Allow 2 inches beyond the seamline where the inside and outside arm panels join. Pin the outside arm panel to the inside arm panel: Starting at the center point of the

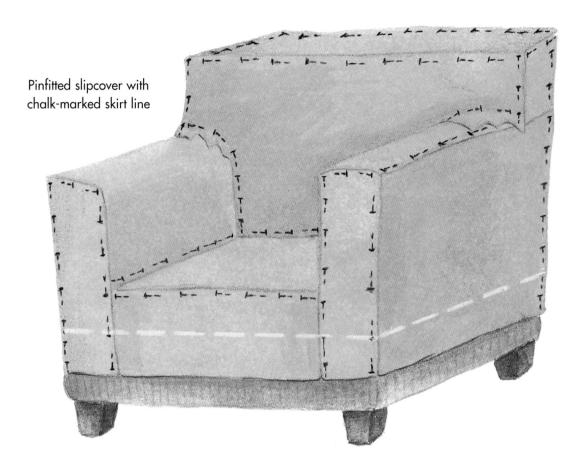

Pinfitted slipcover with chalk-marked skirt line

seam, work first to the arm front then back toward the shoulder, where the seam meets the inside back panel.

5. OUTSIDE BACK (E). The zipper closure on the basic slipcover runs from 2 inches below the upper edge of the chair to the bottom of the slipcover. Pin the outside back panel to the top boxing panel as noted for the inside back panel, then to the shoulder and outside arm panels. Trim the bottom as needed to allow 2 inches below the skirtline.

6. FRONT APRON (F). Pin this panel carefully to the chair front, but not to any other panels at this time.

7. DECK (G). Pin the deck panel to the inside back panel, then to the inside arm panels at the tuck-in allowances. Trim the tuck-in allowances into curves so the allowance is widest at the center of the deck sides and back and tapers to about ¾ inch at the corners. Pin the front edge of the deck panel to the upper edge of the apron panel.

8. FRONT ARM (H). Pin the front arm panel to the inside arm panel: Starting at the center point of the inside arm seamline, pin down to the bottom, then up to the top of the arm. *Note:* As the arm curves, you may need to pin some darts in the inside arm panel. Repeat to pin the front arm panel to the outside arm panel and front apron end, starting just beneath the arm curl.

9. SHOULDER (I). Following the original upholstery seamlines where appropriate, pin the shoulder panel to surrounding panels in this order: top boxing; outside back; and inside back, starting at the center point and working up to the top boxing, then down to the seam joining the inside and outside arms. Pin the remaining panel side, starting at the outside back and working toward the seam joining the inside and outside arms; follow the chalk line, keep the pins parallel to the floor, and stop the pinning about 1½ inches short of completion. Hold together the remaining seam allowances and clip and notch as needed to enable you to pin these sections together, but do not clip or notch any closer than ½ inch from the eventual stitching line. *Note:* The bottom of this panel may end above or below where the original upholstery does, depending on where you made the arm seam. Also, if your chair top back is slightly rounded, you may need to make a small dart angling in from each back corner of the top boxing.

10. CUSHION TOP AND BOTTOM (J). Pin the cushion cover top and bottom panels to the cushion, then use chalk to mark along the existing welting around the cushion perimeter. Unpin the fabric. Use a yardstick to straighten any lines as needed, then cut ½ inch beyond the lines to create a seam allowance. *Note:* The cushion cover boxing strips were cut to size during the blocking process.

11. SKIRT (L). Using a 12-inch ruler, measure up from the floor to the desired finished skirt length; mark that length around all sides of the cover. This will be the skirt seamline. *Note:* The skirt is not pin-fitted to the slipcover; rather, it is added after the slipcover is sewn together. For details on cutting and creating the kick-pleat skirt featured on the basic slipcover, see "Creating and Attaching the Skirt," on page 48. For alternatives refer to "Skirts," on page 56.

Final Adjustments

Before you do the final trimming on the slipcover seam allowances, check all seams carefully to be sure they fit smoothly. Adjust the pinned seamlines as needed for a tight fit and align any stray pins. Then follow these guidelines to trim the pin-fitted slipcover:

• Trim all seam allowances to ½ inch (or ¼ inch in very tight areas), *except* at the tuck-in allowances and the closure seam (along one chair back corner on the featured basic slipcover). *Note:* If you do trim to ¼ inch, when sewing that area shorten the stitch length for a stronger seam.

• Check that all tuck-in allowances taper to ½-inch allowances at corners. Trim the closure seam to ¾ inch (1 inch on bulky fabric), tapering the seam to ½ inch in the 2-inch area from the top of the closure to the top of the slipcover, above where the zipper will be inserted.

• In curved areas or crowded intersections, cut one seam allowance at a time. This will result in more accurate cuts.

• If you need to reclip some areas, be sure not to cut too close to the temporary seamline. When you check the fit with the cover right side out, you may need room to adjust the seamline outward.

• If desired, before removing the cover from the chair, use chalk to mark along pinned seamlines, especially in critical areas such as curves, corners, darts, and closure seams. The marked seamline will be easy to repin if pins come out during removal and sewing. *Note:* If you pin-fitted with the fabric right side out, an easy way to mark the seams is to spread open the seam allowances and run the chalk along the pinned lines.

• You will need to unpin all seams to insert trim and to sew them; if you haven't already done so, identify each panel by chalk-marking an identifier. Also, use a *T* or *F* to indicate the top or front edge of pieces.

• To be sure edges can be perfectly matched, make notches on all the seams, including the tuck-in edges. Space the notches 6 to 7 inches apart on long straight edges and 2 to 4 inches apart on short or curved seams (see **Notching,** on page 106). If you need to distinguish the notches to facilitate matching, make groupings of one, two, or three notches.

• Unpin the closure seam. Remove the T-pins anchoring the slipcover to the upholstery, then remove the slipcover from the chair.

• Carefully turn the slipcover right side out and place it over the chair again. If the cover is too loose or too tight in spots, mark the right side with chalk or pins so you can make the proper adjustments after you remove the cover.

Your slipcover is about to start taking a permanent shape. Continue to be patient through the unpinning and repinning process, and select the options that make the best sense for your project, materials, and desired style.

Sewing the Slipcover

Accenting the Seams

Although welting is the most common seam accent, twisted cord with lip, fringe, rickrack, and other trims can be used creatively to give your slipcover a unique look. Your choice for accenting seams can alter the look of your slipcover, making it dressy or more casual, traditional or more contemporary. For details on an array of choices, see "Trim Options," on page 24, as well as the project instructions in Part 3.

• Remember that contrast trim will define the lines of your furniture, so if you don't want to emphasize the shape, choose a self-fabric or matching color trim.

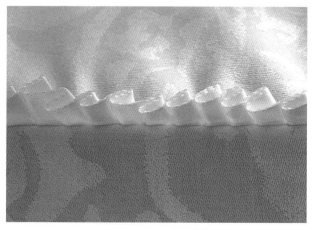

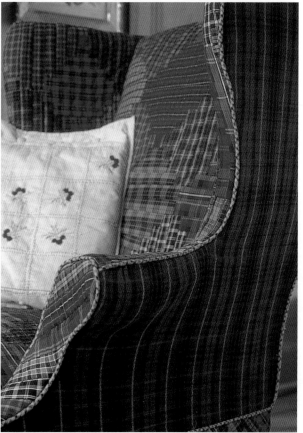

• If you're making your own welting, use fabric set aside before blocking to create the amount of welting you need (which you determine by using a chart or formula in Part 1). For details, see **Welting,** on page 108.

• Before you sew each slipcover seam that requires welting, unpin it and stitch the welting (or other trim) into place. You may find it easier, and faster in the long run, to stitch the trim to one side before sewing the seam together.

LEFT: *Welting is one common way to accent seams. Here a contrast fabric was used to create the welting. Custom-made pleated ribbon (ABOVE) provides a unique alternative. Trims are not the only way to create interest at the seamlines; simple topstitching (ABOVE LEFT) gives a tailored, finished look.*

Controlling Fullness

Several methods control fullness in curved areas. Darts and folds are more tailored than gathers, so the style of the cover may suggest the best method for easing in fullness. See **darts, folds,** and **gathering** in Part 4 for details about these techniques. Sew all darts, folds, or gathers before starting on the seams of the slipcover.

• To create darts, pin fabric layers together up to the curved area. Work from the center out to form tucks that fit the longer edge to the shorter edge. Chalk the dartlines on the wrong side of the fabric, marking over the pins. Remove pins. Refold the dart, right sides together, matching markings. Pin and stitch, sewing from the fabric edge to the dart tip; shorten the stitch length as you come to the tip. Trim the dart allowance to ¼ inch.

• Folds accomplish the same goal as darts, but they are left open. To fit a larger fabric edge to a smaller edge, start in the center of the curve and form equal folds in the larger edge. Once the two edges match, sew the folds inside the seam allowance.

• Gathers are a soft way to control fullness along curves. Various methods can be used to pull up a given length of fabric to measure a smaller distance across, thereby creating soft even pleats. For details, see **Gathering,** on page 106.

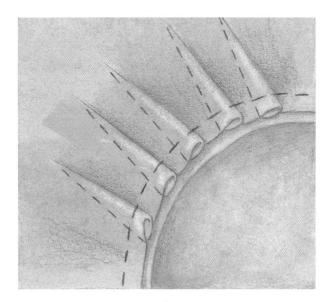

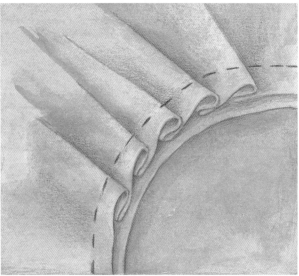

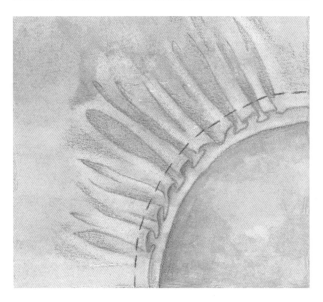

Sewing Sequence

Use this list as a quick reference as you sew your slipcover.

1. Unwelted seams
2. Front apron to deck
3. Top boxing to shoulder panels
4. Inside back to shoulder panels
5. Inside arms to outside arms
6. Inside arms to shoulder panels
7. Front arm panels to inside-outside arms and front apron
8. Outside back to rest of slipcover
9. Skirt
10. Zipper
11. Cushion

Basic Construction

Before beginning to sew your slipcover, review the Sewing Sequence box on page 47 for a quick overview of the order of construction.

1. Sew the unwelted seams first. These usually include the tuck-ins around the three sides of the deck and the **inside arm–inside back** seams.

2. Apply welting to the upper edge of the **front apron** panel, then sew it to the front edge of the **deck** panel.

3. Apply welting to each end of the **top boxing** panel, then sew it to the top of each **shoulder** panel. Press the seams toward the top boxing panel.

4. Apply welting around the **inside back** panel, from where its side meets the arm, across the top, and down the other side to the arm. Then sew welting to the **shoulder** panel, **top boxing,** and **shoulder** panel on the other side. Press the seams toward the shoulder panels.

5. Apply welting to the upper edge of each **outside arm** panel, then sew each **inside arm** panel to the **outside arm** panel and the lower edge of each **shoulder** panel. Press the seams toward the inside arm and shoulder panels.

6. Apply welting to the front edge of each inside-outside arm section, then sew each **front arm** panel to the **inside-outside arm** section and **front apron** panel, upper edge and ends. Press the seam allowances toward the inside-outside arm sections. *Note:* At this point, try the slipcover on the furniture and make any necessary adjustments.

7. Apply welting around the entire back edge of the partially constructed slipcover, starting at the bottom of the **outside arm** panel, up the **shoulder** panel, across the **top boxing** panel, down the other **shoulder** panel, and down to the bottom of the other **outside arm** panel. Then sew the **outside back** panel to the rest of the slipcover, along these same seams, leaving the closure seam unsewn except for 2 inches at the top. Press the seam allowances toward the outside back panel.

8. Try the slipcover on the chair again. Check the skirtline with a ruler; revise the line if needed. Trim the bottom edge seam allowance to ½ inch from the marked chalk line. Cut the welting cord so it is even with the bottom of the closure edges (see **Welting,** on page 108). Apply welting around the skirtline, beginning and ending at the closure edges and removing 1 inch of welting cord at each end. Press the seam allowances at the front arm panels toward the front arms; press outside back–outside arm allowances toward the outside back panel.

Creating and Attaching the Skirt

The featured basic slipcover has a lined skirt with kick pleats at each corner. Because of the corner zipper closure, the pleat at the closure corner zips up the cen-

LEFT: *Once the front arm panel is sewn to its corresponding sections, try the slipcover on and make any necessary adjustments.* OPPOSITE: *A side view of the shoulder panel.*

ter. To make this skirt, use the instructions that follow. *Note:* If the back of your chair will be visible, consider ending the zipper at the skirtline and using a removable mock kick pleat at the closure corner. For basic information on other slipcover skirts and skirt variations, including the mock kick pleat, see "Skirts," on page 56.

1. To determine the cut size for each of the four required skirt panels, first plan your skirt on paper. Each skirt panel width will be a chair side width measurement plus 13 to 17 inches to accommodate one pleat (12 inches for a 3-inch-deep pleat, 16 inches for a 4-inch-deep pleat and two seam allowances). Each skirt panel length will be the desired finished length of the skirt, plus 3 inches for seam allowances and hem. On your plan, note the length of each strip. For an easy way to ensure skirt piecing seams are hidden within pleats, subtract 2 inches from the first panel width and add 2 inches to the last panel width.

2. Cut the fabric strips across the fabric width according to your plan. Also cut lining fabric panels the same width as the skirt face fabric panels but 4 inches shorter in length.

3. Based on your plan, seam the face skirt panel together Eend to end, leaving two ends unseamed. Press the seams open. Repeat for the lining strips.

4. With right sides together, sew the skirt to the lining at one long edge. Press the seams open. Turn the skirt right side out and bring the other long edges together; this will create a hem on the wrong side. Baste the long edges together and press the skirt.

5. Pin the skirt to the slipcover with right sides together and raw edges even, beginning and ending at the slipcover opening edge with a half kick pleat (3 or 4 inches deep, depending on your plan). Then pin the center of each width to the center front, center back, and centers of each side. Carry the fullness between pins to each corner to form a kick pleat at each corner. Be sure the hemlines meet at the base of the zipper opening.

6. Baste the skirt to the slipcover and try it on the chair. Make any needed adjustments, then stitch the skirt into place.

Dressing Your Slipcover

It's payoff time! Your slipcover is completed, and you're ready for the unveiling. To dress your slipcover for success, follow these tips:

• Be sure you've clipped all thread tails and removed all pins.

• Slip the cover over the furniture and gently pull it into place; fasten any closures.

• Use a long-handled wooden spoon to insert tuck-ins into crevices.

• To keep your slipcover from shifting, insert rolled-up newspaper, fabric scraps, or foam strips into the crevices after your tuck-ins are in place. Or purchase vinyl wedges, such as Tuck-Once grips, designed specifically for this purpose.

• Position any cushions with the zipper closure toward the back, and remember to turn the cushions over occasionally to ensure even wear.

Inserting the Zipper Closure

The basic slipcover is secured with a zipper at the back right corner. For basic information on other slipcover closures, such as Velcro fasteners, ties, lacing rhrough grommets, and buttons, see "Closures," on page 61. For sofabed closures, see page 63. *Note:* Reverse the instructions that follow if you're using a back *left* corner closure.

1. At the opening for the zipper, be sure the raw edges of the skirt and slipcover are even.

2. Press under and baste into place the opening seam allowance on the outside back edge (without welting). Press the skirt-slipcover seam allowance toward the slipcover.

3. On the other opening seam allowance (welted edge), position the closed zipper with the tab end ½ inch above the skirt-slipcover lower edge; fold back the zipper tapes as needed. With right sides together, pin the slipcover to the closed zipper so the welting

A completed slipcover outlined in vibrant red welting now dresses the basic chair.

stitching line is ⅛ inch to the left of the zipper teeth; the welting will cover the teeth. Beginning at the skirt-slipcover lower edge and continuing the length of the zipper, use a zipper foot to sew along the welting stitching line.

4. On the outside back opening seam allowance, place the opening fold next to the welting, covering the zipper teeth. Stitch the other zipper half to this side, ½ to ⅝ inch from the folded edge. Stitch across the top edge of the zipper several times.

Sewing the Cushion Cover

The basic slipcover has a traditional boxed cushion cover. During the blocking process, you cut the cushion top and bottom panels and three strips: two zipper strips, one pressed in half lengthwise, and one boxing strip. To create this cushion cover, use the instructions that follow. Cushion preparation and cover types are discussed later in Part 2.

1. Place the two zipper strips right sides together and sew them together along the crease: Begin with a regular stitch for 1 inch, switch to a basting stitch up to 1 inch from the other end, then switch back to regular stitching for the last 1 inch.

2. Press open the zipper strips so the basted-together folds are at the center. Center the zipper face-down over the basted seam; baste into place. Sew the zipper into place across the zipper ends. Remove the basting stitches. The doubled fabric on each side of the zipper adds strength to the construction.

3. Stitch welting to the right sides of the cushion top and bottom panel, joining the ends at the back edges (see **Welting,** on page 108).

4. Mark the center point of the boxing strip, then mark the center point of the cushion top panel, front. With right sides together, pin the boxing strip to the cushion top panel perimeter, matching the center marks and stopping approximately 5 inches from each end; as you come to corners, clip the boxing strip only, not the cushion top panel.

5. With right sides together, center the zipper strip along the cushion top panel, back edge, and pin it to the top to about 2 inches from each end.

6. Pin together the boxing and zipper strip ends at the zipper stopper end so the strips will fit the cushion panels, trimming the boxing strip end seam

allowance to ½ inch. Repeat at the other zipper strip end, this time lapping the boxing strip over the zipper strip end by 1½ inches and trimming away any boxing strip excess. Pin the remainder of the zipper and boxing strip to the cushion top panel, creating a 1-inch tuck at the zipper pull end.

7. Sew the boxing and zipper strip ends together at each end; sew the remainder of the boxing strip to the cushion top panel. *Note:* Be sure the tuck at the zipper pull end is forming correctly as seen from the viewer's side.

8. Open the zipper, then pin and sew the boxing-zipper strip to the bottom panel of the cushion. *Note:* To be sure of a good fit, follow these tips: Fold the boxing-zipper strip at the corners, and clip the seam allowance to mark the lower corners. Align the fold

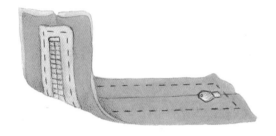

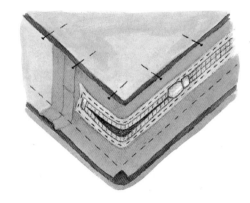

with the clip marks and pin the boxing-zipper strip corner areas to the cushion bottom panel, clipping only the boxing-zipper strip as needed for a smooth fit; baste the corners into place. Check to be sure the corners are perfectly aligned with the top.

9. Turn the cover right side out and insert the filler, stretching the cover from front to back. If using an old cushion filler, fill out any corner gaps with batting. Close the zipper. Smooth the cover over the filler from the center outward.

Slipcover Variations

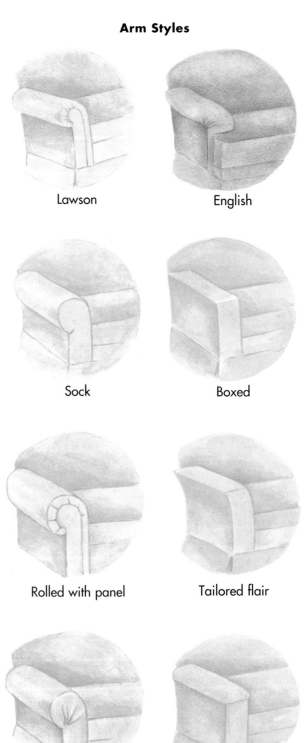

Lawson   English

Sock   Boxed

Rolled with panel   Tailored flair

Rolled with pleats   Cap

ARMS

The component of upholstered furniture that has the greatest variety of shapes is the arm. The arm may come fully to the front of the piece, it may be set back a bit, or it may extend to the front at the same height as the back of the piece. Using the suggestions offered here, you should be able to adapt the basic slipcover instructions to fit any arm situation.

• **ROLLED, SOCK, AND LAWSON ARMS.** Constructed with a shaped front arm panel, these arms allow you to ignore the existing upholstery seams, if desired, to simplify the slipcover.

• **ENGLISH ARMS.** This type of arm is unusual in that it has no separate front panel. Instead, the inside arm panel wraps around the arm front curve to meet the side of the outside arm. Darts, folds, or gathers are used on the inside arm panel and front arm panel curve to shape the piece to meet the outside arm.

• **BOXED, TAILORED FLAIR, AND CAP ARMS.** These types will need a top boxing panel. This means you will have an extra welted seam on the arm, but otherwise the attachment to the outside back and the front arm panel will be similar to that of the basic slipcover.

SHAPED DECK

The basic chair has a simple square deck fitted with a square cushion. Equally common is a T-shaped deck and cushion. The T shape will not affect the construction of the inside and outside arm; what does change is the shape of the deck panel, the length of the front apron panel, and how these two panels join.

Cut the deck panel in the shape of the deck, with the tuck-in allowance extending around the front of the arm up to the outside edge of the chair. Clip the tuck-in allowance at the sharply curved area to within 1 inch of the future seamline. End the outside arm panel at the *arm* front edge, not the *furniture* front edge; extend the front apron panel around the front corners to meet the outside back edge (refer to the photo on page 54).

BACKS

Although backs also come in numerous shapes, there are three basic styles: tight, loose pillow, and semi-attached.

• **TIGHT BACK CONSTRUCTION.** A chair of this type has no back cushion. The chair used in the basic slipcover example is of this type. If a chair with tight back construction has a very narrow back, you can eliminate the top boxing and shoulder panels. Wrap

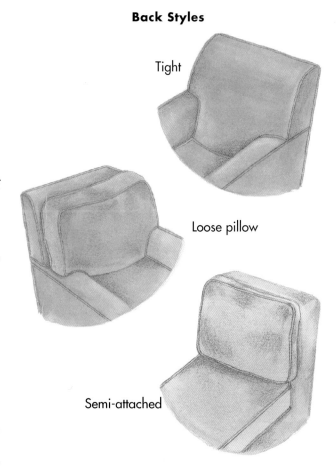

Tight

Loose pillow

Semi-attached

the inside back panel directly to the outside back and sew it directly to the outside back and outside arm panels. Use darts, gathers, or tucks to achieve a good fit in the shaped areas.

• **LOOSE PILLOW BACK CONSTRUCTION.** The distinguishing feature of this type (shown left) is that the back pillow section can be removed and covered in the same fashion as the seat cushion. For the panel behind the loose pillow, use tight back construction, with or without a top boxing panel as needed.

• **SEMI-ATTACHED BACK CONSTRUCTION.** This kind of chair has a pillow that looks loose but is not. Three sides of the back have crevices that separate the cushion from the back. If the chair back and the pillow back are even, fill the crevices with batting—using a curved upholstery needle to baste the batting to the upholstery—and proceed as for a tight back with top boxing. If the two sections are at different levels, however, slipcovering is very difficult, and I do not recommend it.

CUSHIONS

Most chair and sofa cushions fall into three basic categories: traditional boxed, soft-corner boxed, and mitered corner. For your slipcover, choose the style that best mirrors your current cushions or change the look of your furniture by selecting a different cushion style. Refer to "Blocking" on page 40 and "Sewing the Cushion Cover" on page 51.

Traditional Boxed Cushion Cover

The cushions on most upholstered furniture feature a 2- to 4-inch-wide insert strip. Usually called boxing, this strip joins the cushion top and bottom panels and its height determines the cushion's depth. The cushion may be square or rectangular, T-shaped, oval, or some variation thereof.

Soft-Corner Boxed Cushion Cover

On this cushion type, the front edges are rounded and the top and bottom panels are made from one panel of fabric. The boxing is formed by inset strips on three sides. This easy cover works well on square or rectangular cushions that are slightly worn along the front

edges. For this style, avoid fabrics with a pattern that has to be centered on the cover top, bottom, or front edge. Welting is not generally used on soft-corner boxed cushions, though it can be added to the seams if desired. *Note:* If you're not removing the old cover from a conventionally boxed cushion, cut away any welting from the old cover, cutting *above* the stitching line.

1. Cut the top, bottom, and front boxed edges of this cushion as a single panel. To determine its dimensions, measure from the cushion top, back edge, down around the front edge, and back along the bottom to the back edge. Measure the cushion width across the top. Cut a rectangular panel using these measurements, adding a ½-inch seam allowance all around.

2. Fold the rectangular panel in half widthwise; mark the midpoint at each end of the fold. Pin the rectangular panel to the cushion top, front, and bottom, matching the midpoint markings to the front center of the cushion's depth. If the rectangle is a little long, trim the back edges to maintain a ½-inch seam allowance.

3. To cut and prepare the boxing and zipper strip, follow the instructions for the basic slipcover's traditional boxed cushion; refer to "Blocking," on page 38, and "Sewing the Cushion Cover," on page 51, but calculate for boxing only the side and back edges.

4. Fold the side boxing strips in half lengthwise and mark the midpoint. Round the strip ends above and below this mark to create a softly rounded front edge. With the rectangular panel in place around the cushion, pin-fit these boxing strips to the cushion cover, matching the midpoints.

5. Matching the center back of the rectangle to the center of the zipper strip, lengthwise, pin the zipper strip around the back and sides of the cushion and pin it to the side boxing strips where they meet.

6. Notch the zipper strip and rectangle as needed along one seam edge; to remove the cushion unpin that area and remove the cover. Open the zipper before repinning that area, matching notches. Sew the boxing and zipper strips to the rectangle.

OPPOSITE, FAR LEFT: *T-shaped deck and cushion.*
OPPOSITE, NEAR LEFT: *Traditional boxed cushions.*
ABOVE: *A single traditional boxed cushion is outlined in bushy fringe.*

Cushion Basics

- Most furniture cushion forms are foam rubber or have a foam core wrapped with polyester batting. On expensive furniture you may find down cushions, but even those cushions often have a foam or spring core.

- Replace cushion fillers if the existing filler has turned to yellow dust, smells bad, or makes a cracking sound when folded. Replacement is also recommended if the cushion is misshapen or if the front edges are rounded or more compressed than the rest of the cushion.

- To create replacement cushion fillings: Select a high-density, firm foam for seat cushions and a softer, less dense foam for back cushions. Draw the existing cushion shape on the foam, adding 1 inch on all sides for a snug fit. Cut out the cushion with an electric carving knife or ask your supplier to cut it for you. To give your new cushion form a soft, crowned appearance, wrap the foam with a layer of ½-inch upholstery batting. Secure the batting to the foam with special foam adhesive or large basting stitches. Do not put any batting in the zipper area.

- If you decide not to replace the cushion filling, enhance the cushion's appearance by making the new cushion cover smaller than the original (eliminating seam allowances works well), resulting in a slightly snugger fit, or by wrapping the old cushion with upholstery batting. To plump a down cushion, cover the down filler with a new muslin cover and add layers of polyester batting, polyester stuffing, or more down. If only the front edges of the cushion form are worn, consider changing the cushion style to soft-corner construction.

- A zipper is the best closure for cushions. For cushions that are concealed on three sides, the zipper strip should extend across the back and 2 to 4 inches around each back corner. For mitered box cushions or cushions that will be exposed on three sides, cut the zipper strip 3 inches shorter than the back edge of the cushion.

- When working with striped, plaid, or large-motif fabric, match the cushion top and bottom panels to the slipcover. For details, see Patterned Slipcover, on page 72, and Perfect Placement, on page 22.

- To make it easier to insert the foam cushion form into the cover, make a muslin cover for the filler or wrap the filler with a thin dry-cleaner's bag for insertion, removing it afterward.

Mitered-Corner Cushion Cover

Also called a mock box, this cushion cover has the depth of a boxed cushion cover but no inset strip; the boxing is created by mitering the top and bottom panel corners. The mitered corners can be stitched, left unstitched, or butterflied for even softer corners. Welting is usually inserted in the seams that run around the cushion, but seams can be left unwelted.

1. Wrap a tape measure around the cushion form lengthwise, then widthwise, noting these measurements, then dividing them by 2. Cut two panels, using these halved measurements as dimensions, plus ½ inch all around for seam allowances. Also measure and note the cushion depth.

2. On each edge of the cover panels, measure in from the corners half the cushion depth plus ½ inch. Make a mark at this point.

3. Using these markings, fold each corner diagonally with right sides together. Align the raw edges and markings; pin each panel. *For stitched corners:* Sew from the marking to the folded edge. *For unstitched corners:* Sew in from the marking ½ inch, securing the stitch-

ing ends well. *For butterflied corners:* Stitch as for unstitched corners, then pull down the loose fabric tongue at the folded edge, bringing it no more than ½ inch beyond the seam allowance, and tack it into place.

4. Place the two mitered panels, right sides together, over the cushion filler. Pin the edges together to check the fit.

5. Unpin the layers and remove them from the filler. Repin and sew them together along the back edge and halfway down each side. At each corner, fold the fabric ears in opposite directions or cut away the excess fabric if desired. Insert a zipper in the back seam.

6. Open the zipper and pin and sew the rest of the cover together. Turn the cover right side out and insert the filler.

SKIRTS

Slipcovers can have skirts even if the furniture they cover does not; indeed, a skirt often improves the appearance of a piece of furniture. When choosing a skirt style for your slipcover, keep in mind the fact that the skirt will define your slipcover perhaps more than any other feature. Use the tips below and the specific skirt instructions in this section to help you choose the skirt that's right for your project.

• Skirts are functional as well as fashionable: Their weight helps to stabilize and keep the slipcover in place.

• Choose a skirt style that is in keeping with the style of the room for which the furniture is intended. For example, gathers give soft, graceful lines; pleats create a crisp, formal effect. And remember: Having no skirt at all is also an option, for contemporary, spare-looking slipcovers, or if you wish to expose the wooden legs.

• Consider your fabric when making a skirt selection. Patterned fabrics may be more suitable for certain skirt styles. For example, it may be difficult to match the stripes on a pleated skirt to those on the slipcover; a gathered style would not present a matching problem.

• On flat-style skirts, take care to match any patterns on the skirt front; mismatches on the sides and back will be less noticeable.

• No seams should be visible on the skirt front

panel. Hide seams in pleats or gathers, even if it means extra yardage.

- Although **railroading** (see page 107) isn't recommended for a slipcover body, it can cut down on piecing seams for the skirt, especially with solid fabrics. For certain fabrics, such as those featuring lengthwise stripes, railroading also offers the opportunity to showcase a select portion of a print.

Skirt Preparation

Use these tips in determining the cut size of skirt panels:

- The skirt should always be the same finished height from the floor on all sides, regardless of the furniture's slants and slopes, and should just clear the floor.
- Placement of the skirtline is personal preference. Use these basic guidelines and your eye to help you choose the optimal height from the floor: standard placement, 7 to 8 inches; dressmaker style, 10 inches; waterfall style, directly from the deck. Whatever you choose, be sure the seamline for the skirt falls above any welting line on the upholstered piece.
- The most accurate measurements come from making a template. To make one, wrap around the piece of furniture a long strip of muslin (2 to 4 inches

OPPOSITE: *A cushion with mitered corners on a loose back sofa.* ABOVE: *Detail of kick pleated skirt.* RIGHT: *Mock kick pleat.*

wide) or adding machine tape. Mark on it the corners and location of any pleats or decorative elements. Unless obvious, mark corresponding spots on the slipcover. Where the opening will be, add extra for seam allowances.

- Refer to "Determining Fabric Yardage," on page 20, for basic yardage formulas for different skirt styles.

Straight or Tailored Skirt

This easiest, most popular style features kick pleats at corners and, on larger pieces, at the center as well. For details on this skirt style, which is featured in the basic slipcover, see "Creating and Attaching the Skirt," on page 48. For two variations on this style—mock kick pleats and box pleats—see the details that follow.

- MOCK KICK PLEATS. Created by using separate flaps behind skirt sections that meet at furniture corners, the result is almost identical to that of a skirt with full kick pleats. This style is especially appropriate for showing a contrast fabric peeking out at each corner, dealing with bulky fabric, or concealing the zipper closure when the back of the slipcover will show. To make mock kick pleats:

1. Cut four flap pieces 7 to 9 inches wide by the length of your chosen skirt plus ½-inch seam allowance all around. From lining fabric, cut four flap lining pieces 1 inch narrower and ½ inch shorter than the face fabric flaps. *Note:* You'll need also one piece of Velcro fastener tape as long as the flap finished width. You will use the tape to attach the opening corner flap.

2. Sew lining to each skirt panel and flap, right sides together. Turn the skirt panels and flaps right side out; press.

3. Pin the skirt sections to the slipcover, right sides together, making sure the hems meet exactly at the corners and zipper opening. Stitch the skirt sections into place.

4. Center and pin a flap over the skirt ends at each corner except the opening corner. *Note:* Position the flaps so they are ⅛ to ¼ inch shorter than the skirt so the flap corners won't extend below the skirt. Sew the three flaps to the cover.

5. Insert a zipper at the slipcover opening with the tab positioned at the skirtline instead of the skirt hemline, or apply Velcro fastener tape along the opening, beginning at the skirtline as described in "Closures," on page 61.

6. Cut a length of Velcro fastener tape as long as the remaining flap is wide. Stitch the Velcro loop portion at the right side, upper edge, of the tab. Cut the hook portion in half and stitch half to each side of the zipper closure corner at the skirtline, on the wrong side of the slipcover.

7. Put the slipcover on the chair and zip the closure. Press the remaining flap into place.

• **BOX PLEATS.** Choose box pleats to create formal appeal and a dramatic change from basic kick pleats or gathers. However, box pleats require substantial preplanning and the use of a template as described in "Skirt Preparation," on page 57. Although the instructions that follow are for an unlined hem, it can be lined by using the same concepts detailed in the basic slipcover instructions (see "Additional Calculations," on page 21, and "Creating and Attaching the Skirt," on page 48).

1. Determine the skirt length by using the method under "Additional Calculations," on page 21.

2. To determine skirt width, first determine the number, size, and spacing of skirt pleats. Measure the width of one side and the front or back of your furniture, then determine a number by which both measurements are evenly divisible. For example, a chair with 30-inch-wide sides and a 36-inch-deep front and back could have 6-inch pleats on all sides—five pleats on the sides and six pleats on the front and back, with all pleat edges butting. If your measurements can't be evenly divided by desired pleat size, choose one of the following remedies: Modify pleat size as needed, choose the next closest number of whole pleats and manipulate the size of a couple of pleats slightly to accommodate the difference, or consider leaving small spaces between your pleats (you will need to revise the number of pleats to do this). When you've determined pleat size, number, and spacing (if any), add to the furniture perimeter measurement appropriate allowances for all pleats plus ½ inch for each seam allowance.

3. Using a muslin strip or adding machine tape, create a full-sized template for the skirt by wrapping it around the chair or sofa. Mark the pleat folds and, if appropriate, the spacing between them. Use this template to cut and mark the skirt strips. Adjust the skirt strip lengths or pleat size slightly to hide any piecing seams inside a pleat.

4. Join the skirt strips and finish the hem edge (refer to "Hems and Hem Embellishments," on page 60).

5. Lay the template over the wrong side of the skirt and transfer the template markings to the skirt.

6. Form and pin the pleats according to your markings; baste them into place.

7. With right sides together, pin the skirt to the slipcover, matching the corners. Adjust the pleats if necessary. Unpin the skirt and press the pleats well; or for a softer look, leave the pleats unpressed.

8. Sew the skirt to the slipcover.

*Three more skirt options: Straight skirt, here with shaped hem (*OPPOSITE TOP*), box pleats (*LEFT*), and gathered corners (*RIGHT*).*

Gathered Skirt

This lined skirt type will add a romantic touch to a slipcover and is perfect for transforming tailored furniture into more casual pieces. It's easy to make using any of several gathering techniques. *Note:* For a more tailored look, decrease fullness and create a skirt with gathers at each corner only.

1. Determine the skirt length and width by using the method under "Additional Calculations," on page 21, and cut strips for the skirt and lining.

2. Seam the skirt and lining strips and sew the two together as described for the basic slipcover in "Creating and Attaching the Skirt," on page 48.

3. Divide and mark the skirt strip into four sections, proportioned to the length of each side; mark the center of each section. (If your sofa is 36 × 84 inches and the gathered skirt is to be double fullness, you will allow 72 inches for each side and 168 inches for the skirt front and back.)

4. Gather the skirt to achieve the finished skirt length (see **Gathering,** on page 105).

5. With right sides together, pin the skirt to the slipcover. Match the section marks to the skirt corners and each center mark to the center of the appropriate side. Distribute the fullness evenly on each side, leaving some extra fullness in the corners.

6. When stitching the skirt to the slipcover, sew with the skirt underneath and the slipcover on top.

Faced "No-Skirt" Finish

If you want your slipcover to have an upholstered look or you're short on fabric, finish the lower edge of the slipcover with welting and a simple facing cut from the face fabric. Be sure the slipcover-facing seamline is even with the lower edge of the furniture.

1. For each slipcover side, cut a facing piece 3½ inches deep by the width of the side between the legs, plus 2 inches for hem allowance.

2. Sew doubled ½-inch hems on one long and both short ends.

3. Sew welting around the slipcover at the lower edge of the seamline. With right sides together and raw edges even, pin and stitch the facings to the slipcover, leaving space for a leg at each corner.

4. In the unfaced leg areas of the slipcover, clip the seam allowances; turn the allowances to the wrong side of the slipcover and whipstitch them into place.

5. Secure the facings to the furniture underside in one of two ways: Cut Velcro fastener tape lengths the width of each facing piece; sew one portion to the wrong side of the facing in the hem area, and tack the other portion to the wooden frame of the furniture underside. Or use small brads, staples, or upholstery tacks to secure the facing to the frame. *Note:* Although the latter method makes cleaning more troublesome, it is more suitable for pieces with curved bottom edges. In curved areas, fold over and tack down any excess fabric.

HEMS AND HEM EMBELLISHMENTS

The hem edge on the slipcover skirt can add pizzazz to the slipcover's overall appearance. You will find a number of possibilities, from simple to ornate, throughout this book; some are detailed in the list that follows. But there are more—just use your imagination!

- **BASIC DOUBLED HEM.** Press under ¼ to 1 inch twice; topstitch close to the first fold.

- **DOUBLE TOPSTITCHING.** Add a sporty touch by using a double needle to create perfectly spaced rows of machine topstitching. Use a contrast color or buttonhole twist to accentuate the stitching.

- **OVERCAST STITCHING, OR SADDLESTITCHING.** Work this classic handstitch from left to right (or the opposite), bringing the needle through at an acute angle and taking the thread over the edge.

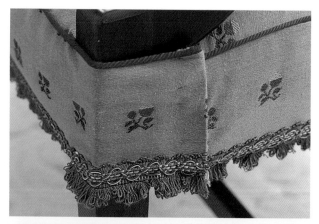

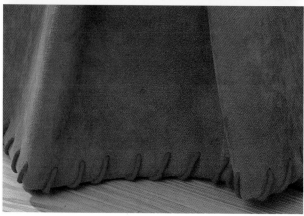

- **BINDING.** Encase the raw edges in a triple-folded fabric strip cut on the straight or bias grain. Choose prefolded bias binding or make your own.

- **BAND TRIM.** Attach this flat, wide trim over a basic doubled hem. Align its bottom edge with the skirt hemline or set it away from the edge a bit. Edgestitch it into place; or for an easy, no-pucker application, adhere it by using fabric glue or iron-on fusible web tape.

- **CORD WITH LIP.** On a straight-style skirt, catch the lip of this twisted cord in a seam that joins a facing to a hem. The result is a crisp, defined edge.

- **FRINGE.** Topstitch the heading of this historically popular trim—whether basic, bullion, or ball—over the slipcover hem to create a rich, elegant effect.

CLOSURES

A zipper is the traditional slipcover closure of choice; it's unobtrusive and offers an easy method for getting the slipcover on and off. For that reason it is the closure method detailed in the basic slipcover technique. However, a distinctive closure can be the finishing touch that gives your slipcover a custom-made, high-style look. Other easily concealed closures include Velcro hook-and-loop fastener tape, snaps, and snap tape. Your slipcover closure needn't be purely functional—ties, lacing through grommets, and buttons are fashionable alternatives. Following are instructions for installing these slipcover closures, including details

OPPOSITE, TOP TO BOTTOM: *Faced finish with fringe, basic hem, ribbon band trim, and overcast stitching.*
ABOVE: *Bias fabric binding.* RIGHT: *Zipper.*

about how to modify the basic slipcover to accommodate them.

Velcro and Snap Tape

Velcro is the most common brand of hook-and-loop fastener tape. The $\frac{3}{4}$-inch-wide Velcro tape most appropriate for slipcovers can be purchased prepackaged or by the yard and is commonly available in white and black, but may be found in other colors. To use Velcro tape instead of a zipper, follow the instructions that follow. *Note:* To use $\frac{1}{2}$-inch-wide snap tape instead, follow the same instructions, substituting the socket portion for the Velcro hook portion and the ball portion for the loop portion.

1. Purchase fastener yardage equal to the length of the slipcover opening.

2. Leave 1-inch seam allowances at the slipcover opening seam (including the skirt ends, if applicable). Serge or zigzag the opening edges before constructing the slipcover.

3. Topstitch the Velcro hook portion to the outside back opening seam allowance *right* side, with the Velcro inner edge just inside the seamline; stitch through the seam allowance only.

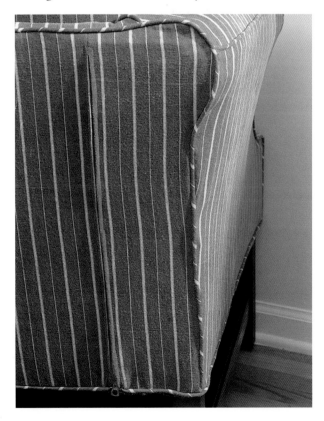

4. Press under the seam allowance on the other (welted) opening seam allowance, and sew the Velcro loop portion to that seam allowance *right* side.

5. Complete the slipcover and place it on the furniture; allow the welted seam allowance to extend around to the chair back at the opening corner. Turn under the Velcro hook portion and press it firmly onto the loop portion.

Ties

Ties can be beautiful, whimsical, or understated—depending on the material you use—and can be positioned at one or more corners or the center back of your slipcover. Make spaghetti ties (see **Spaghetti Tie,** on page 108) or wide ties from the slipcover or welting fabric. Or select unusual tie materials—diaphanous ribbon, silky cord, even rustic jute—depending on the look and feel you want.

1. Create or cut ties as needed, checking that they are the appropriate length for their intended use. Finish each end with seam sealant or a knot to keep the exposed cut end from fraying or raveling.

2. Create seams in which to insert your ties. For corner ties, cut 3-inch-wide facings to attach to the existing seam allowances at the opening corner(s). Or create an opening at the center back by cutting the back panel in two sections and creating 3-inch-wide facings to seam to the center opening seam allowances.

3. Clean-finish all facing edges, except those that will be joined to the slipcover opening edges.

4. Pin and sew the facings to the opening edges,

with the right sides together and the ties positioned as desired in between.

5. To keep the upholstery fabric from showing through the small gaps between the ties, create from the slipcover fabric a **clean-finished** (see page 104) rectangle that is large enough to cover the exposed area. Attach the rectangle along the length of the seam allowance.

Lacing Through Grommets

A grommet-and-tie lace-up creates a focal point at the center back, making it ideal for a slipcover whose back will show.

1. As you block a pinfit the outside back, plan a box pleat with a 3-inch return in the center of the panel.

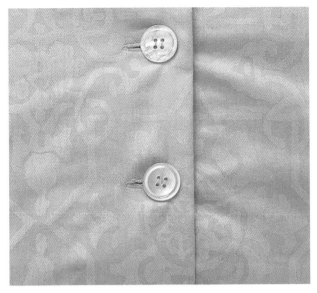

2. The grommets are installed through the face fabric and facing return only; the pleat back covers the upholstery so that there are no gaps between the grommets.

3. Mark the placement of the grommets with chalk or air-soluble marker and insert following the package directions.

4. You may find it easier to lace the panels together before continuing construction, being careful not to catch the ends of the tie in the seam.

Buttons

A button-up closure can be a focal point if desired. Cover self-cover buttons in the slipcover or welt fabric, or select decorative buttons that complement and enhance the slipcover. *Note:* Be sure to choose buttons that are large enough to be in scale with the size of your piece. For instructions, see page 77, step 3.

Sofa Bed Closure

Because a sofa bed must allow access to the bed inside without your having to remove the entire slipcover, a sofa bed presents a special closure challenge. The solution is using two closures, usually zippers. The zippers extend from the floor, up the front skirt and apron, and along the inside arm–deck crevice to the inside back.

1. When you block and pin-fit the slipcover, plan for the front apron panel and the skirt to have zippered openings that run down to the floor from the point where the inside arm meets the deck. Allow at least ¾-inch seam allowances at these openings. If you have a T-shaped deck, you will need to add a small rectangular panel to each corner, at the arm fronts.

2. Construct the slipcover as described in Slip-covering Wide Furniture, on page 41.

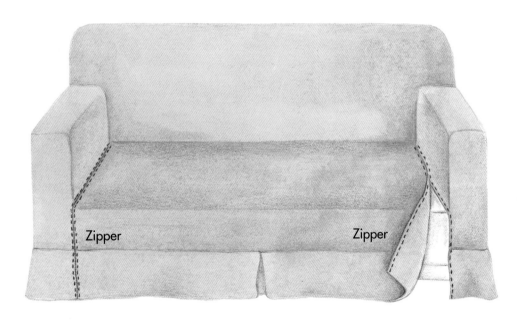

OPPOSITE: *Velcro closures* (TOP LEFT) *are neat and invisible. Spaghetti ties* (TOP RIGHT) *or laced grommets* (BELOW RIGHT) *add a decorative touch.* TOP: *Simple buttons can be demure or dramatic, as you choose.* ABOVE: *Sofabed closure.*

Slipcover Projects

Parts 1 and 2 looked at all angles of the basic upholstered chair slipcover, a true decorating mainstay. But *dozens* of other pieces are well suited to slipcovers. These "alternatives" are explored here. You'll find real-life examples of the specialty slipcover treatments mentioned in Part 1, such as using a quilt as fabric, matching and centering a patterned fabric, and working with exposed wood chair frames. This gallery of 15 slipcover projects (many have patterns included) offers designs that break the slip-cover mold and excite the senses with new possibilities.

How to Use This Section

Most projects in this section are easy enough for a beginner, and all are designed for common pull-up chairs you probably have in your home: The ubiquitous folding chair, the spare director's chair, the regal Queen Anne chair, the quirky butterfly chair, and a wide selection of others all go to slipcover school. And they come out smart and chic, thanks to many of the clever fabric choices and embellishments overviewed in Parts 1 and 2.

Making the Projects in This Section

To make the most of the projects featured from here to page 97, keep in mind the following tips and suggestions:

• **ENLARGE PATTERNS.** The patterns for the projects in this part are offered in one of two different ways: drawn to scale on a grid for you to enlarge or as general shaping guidelines that involve making a template from your own chair (these have no grid). When enlarging or creating patterns and templates, be sure to transfer or make all appropriate markings and notches on your pattern pieces. See **Enlarging Patterns and Diagrams,** on page 105, and **Template,** on page 108.

• **MAKE A MUSLIN.** The slipcovers in this part are designed for specific types of chairs, such as Parsons, ladderback, etc., but chairs may vary from manufacturer to manufacturer. To ensure a perfect fit, I suggest you create a muslin of the cover before you cut the actual slipcover from your chosen fabric, and make any necessary adjustments to the pattern pieces.

• **CONSIDER A LINING.** Unlike slipcovers for upholstered furniture, which do not lend themselves to attached linings (skirts are the exception), a slip-cover for a pull-up chair may require an attached lining. If your chosen fabric is so lightweight or light colored that you can see through it, plan to cut identical fabric and lining pieces, pin them together, and sew them as one.

• **ADD WELTING WITH CARE.** If you plan to add welting to any of the projects, you may need to use special techniques to keep seams flat and reduce bulk. See **Welting,** on page 108.

• **KNOW YOUR HEM OPTIONS.** The hem edge of most of the chair covers in this part can be finished in more than one way. To alter the supplied patterns to accommodate your hem of choice, cut off or add to the hem allowance, being careful to change all affected pattern pieces. *Note:* A turned-up hem calls for a 2-inch hem allowance: Clean-finish the raw edges with a zigzag or three-thread serger stitch, or press under ½ inch; sew the hem into place by hand or machine. A band-trimmed or bias binding–trimmed hem uses an attached fabric piece to finish the edge: Trim away the hem allowance at the hemline; if the cover has a shaped hem, the band will be easier to apply if the fabric is cut on the bias. For more details, see **Banding,** on page 102, and **Binding,** on page 104.

PREVIOUS PAGE: *This has become affectionately known as the "chair" chair. Chairs marching strategically all over a chair add whimsy to a tight back English-arm lounge chair. The Greek key band trim at the hem allowed us to perfectly expose two rows of assorted chairs and cover the tops of the third row.* RIGHT: *The bias binding at the bottom of the chair skirt is cut from the silk used to welt at the seams of the slipcover.*

FRENCH CHAIR

Spaghetti ties attach separate back, seat, and arm covers to expose the wood frame of the chair. The quilting pattern was created to duplicate the lattice design of the gazebo wallpaper.

MATERIALS

* 1¾ yards main fabric
* ½ yard contrast fabric for welting and buttons
* ¾ yard lining
* 1¼ yards fleece batting
* Optional: Five ¾-inch self-cover buttons
* 3½ yards welting cord (⁵⁄₃₂ inch)

YARDAGE AND CUTTING

1. Make templates of the back, seat, and upholstered arm area, (see **Template,** on page 108). On the back piece, plan to cover all the caning and only part of the wood. The pattern illustration gives you an idea about the general shape that your pieces should have. The arm piece is a rectangle that you will shape with darts.

2. Trace the shapes of the back and seat pieces onto a large piece of lining fabric. Enlarge the shapes by ¾ inch all around (½-inch seam allowance plus ¼ inch for quilting take-up). Select a design for the quilting and draw it on the lining fabric, extending the lines a bit beyond the shapelines. Cut pieces of face fabric and batting the same size as the marked lining piece. For the back of the chair back piece, cut an additional piece of face fabric the size of the enlarged template.

3. For the arm covers, mark and undo the darts (see **Dart,** on page 105). Adjust template so that it has a regular shape and the darts are all the same length and depth. Add ½-inch seam allowance all around. Cut face, two lining pieces, and batting the same size as the template for each cover.

4. For the seat skirt pieces, cut strips of face fabric the desired finished width times 2, plus 1 inch for seam allowance. To determine the cut length needed for each side, mea-sure each side of the template, adding 2 inches for turning in at each end. Cut four batting strips the finished depth of the skirt and the template length of the corresponding side.

5. For the ties, cut bias- or straight-grain strips, 1½ inches wide (see **Bias Strip,** on page 102). For the chair back, cut four strips 36 inches long; the seat, eight strips 21 inches; and the arms, eight strips 10 inches.

SEWING INSTRUCTIONS
Chair Back

1. To quilt the chair back piece, sandwich and pin the batting between the wrong sides of the face fabric and the lining piece upon which the design was drawn. Sew along the drawn design lines from the lining side, starting at the center of the design and working outward. When the quilting is complete, cut the piece to the size of the enlarged template.

2. Make 4½ yards of welting from the contrast fabric (see **Welting,** on page 108). Apply welting around the quilted piece, placing the joined ends at the bottom.

3. With right sides together, pin and then sew the other face fabric piece to the quilted one, leaving an opening along the bottom for turning. Trim seam allowance to ¼ inch and notch out excess fabric in curved areas if needed.

4. Turn the piece right side out and press.

5. To make ties, fold the cut strips in half lengthwise, right sides together. Sew the strips, right sides together, ⅜ inch from the folded edge, finishing off one end. Turn right side out; do not press. Finish raw end.

6. Fold strip in half and position the fold at the circles on the wrong side of the chair back at the "ditch" between the

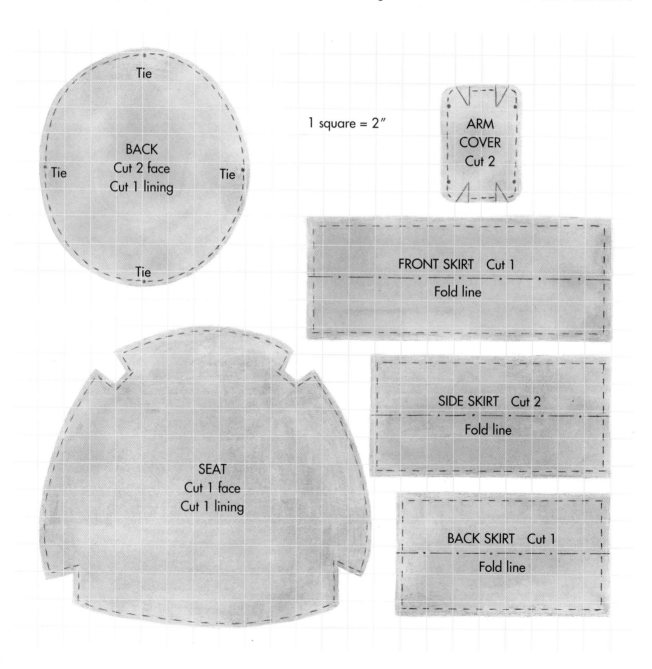

face fabric and the welting. Sew into place by sewing in the ditch. The circles are positioned at the center top and just above the arms.

7. Cover buttons with contrast fabric and sew to the back piece at appropriate locations.

8. To place the tie on the chair, slip one end of the tie through the caning to the back; the other end goes over the wood. Tie the ends in a bow.

Seat

1. Quilt the seat in the same manner as the chair back.

2. To finish the arm and back support cutouts, cut out four 5-inch squares of face fabric for the corner facings. With right sides together, pin a square at each of the cutouts, aligning the raw edges of the squares with the edges of the seat. Stitching from the quilted side of the seat, sew around the cutout sections, providing ½-inch seam allowance. Use very small stitches in the corners. Trim away extra facing fabric in the corners, leaving the ½-inch seam allowance. Clip through the seam allowance, close to the corner stitching. Clean-finish the facing edges. Press the facing to the wrong side of the seat and handstitch into place.

3. Apply welting to the four long edges, stopping and starting the welting at the chair support cutouts.

4. To make the skirt pieces, press each long strip in half lengthwise. Press in 1 inch on each end of the strip. Pin and baste the corresponding batting strip to one side of the folded strip, with one edge of the batting at the foldline; slip the ends of the batting under the turned-under ends of fabric. The batting should fall short of the ½-inch seam allowance at the top of the strip. Press under a ½-inch seam allowance on the unbatted side of the strip.

5. Make ties as in Step 5 of the sewing instructions for the chair back, leaving an unfinished end. Tuck that unfinished end into the fold at each end of the skirt strips. Pin ties into place.

6. With right sides together, pin and then sew the batting side only of each strip to the corresponding side of the seat.

7. Turn the seat over to the wrong side. Pin the unbatted side over the sewn seam allowance, its folded edge meeting the the sewn seam. Hand-sew into place.

8. On the wrong side of the skirt pieces, draw the desired quilting design, being sure to include in that design the closing of the strips at each end and the stitching that anchors the tie in place. Stitch the design.

Arms

1. On the lining fabric, draw a simple quilting design consistent with the quilting on the cover.

2. On the face and lining fabrics, make the darts. On the batting, cut out the dart areas.

3. Pin the batting to the wrong side of the face fabric, positioning the batting around the darts. Baste batting into place.

4. Apply remaining welting around the arm pieces. Make the ties as in Step 5 of the instructions for the seat. Position the ties at circles around the arm piece.

5. With the right side of face fabric to the design side of the lining piece, sew around the arm piece, leaving an opening for turning.

6. Turn right side out; close opening. From the lining side, stitch the design.

WING CHAIR FROM QUILT

A twin-sized quilt is used as the dominant fabric on this wing chair, with the outside back and sides cut from a coordinating plaid. The chair shape is further defined by contrast welting cut from yet another plaid fabric.

MATERIALS

* One twin quilt for inside back, inside arms, inside wings, front apron, front arm panels, cushion, and trim around bottom of chair

* Coordinating fabric for outside arms, outside wings, and outside back

* Contrast fabric for welting and spaghetti ties

* Scraps from any of the fabrics, to be used for the deck

Note: Most wing chairs do not have top boxing; the wings replace the shoulder panels. A skirt can be added if desired.

YARDAGE AND CUTTING

1. Block out all the main pieces as outlined in "Blocking: General Guidelines," on page 38. The smaller pieces—front arm panels, wings, front apron—can be cut from scraps.

2. The inside and outside wings should be blocked out at least 5 inches wider than the wing's greatest width and at least 4 inches longer than the wing's greatest height. The inside wings must match one another and coordinate with the inside back. Outside wings and arms need not match, since you never see both sides at once.

3. Allow for tuck-in where the wing joins the inside back if there is a crevice there. Measure the depth of the crevice with a ruler and add seam allowance.

4. Plan to use scraps for the border at the bottom of the chair.

5. Review "Pin-Fitting: General Guidelines," on page 43.

6. Pin-fit the inside back, followed by the inside arm and outside arm. Make clips in the inside arm seam allowance to fit it around the shaped areas.

7. Pin the inside wing to the upholstery. Remember to allow for tuck-in between the inside wing and the inside back.

8. Pin-fit the inside wing to the outside wing, starting from the midpoint, working down to the bottom, and then up to the top. Follow the upholstery seams for the slipcover seams. You will probably need to use darts to shape the upper portion of the inside wing.

9. Pin-fit the bottom of the inside wing to the top of the inside arm. Clip as needed to get a snug fit.

SEWING INSTRUCTIONS

1. Sew any darts (see **Dart,** on page 105).

2. Sew bottom of inside wing to top of inside arm; include welting (see **Welting,** on page 108).

3. With spring-edge T-deck, sew the tuck-in seam at the front edge and continue the seam along the inside arm–deck to the inside back; no welting.

4. Sew front apron to the deck; welting is optional.

5. Sew outside arm to front arm panel; include welting.

6. Sew inside wing to outside wing, from bottom to top; include welting.

7. Sew outside wing to outside arm, continuing the seam to join the outside arm to the top of the inside arm; include welting.

8. Sew inside wing to inside back. With tuck-in allowance, you can add welt from the top of the chair to the beginning of the tuck-in. Without a tuck-in, add welting along the length of the seam.

9. After all the seams on the front and sides of the slipcover have been sewn, sew the outside arm, outside wing, and inside back to the outside back, leaving a corner open for the closure; include welting.

10. Top-apply strips of the quilt around the bottom edge of the chair, and on the sides and back. See "Skirts," on page 56.

11. Closure: Cut and make spaghetti ties (see **Spaghetti Tie,** on page 108). Position ties along the closure opening. Cut facing pieces the length of the opening; pin and sew one on each side. Turn in and press facing; sew into place by hand. Make a flap piece that will fall behind the opening to conceal the upholstery in the spaces between the ties. Attach the flap along the length of the seam allowance. For more detailed instructions on how to create this closure, see **Ties,** on page 62.

PATTERNED SLIPCOVER

Fabrics with large, dominant motifs can make stunning slipcovers but require extra yardage, careful planning, and a good understanding of the slipcover process. It is best for beginners to avoid using large prints until one or two projects are completed successfully.

MATERIALS

* Fabric as calculated for a tailored skirt in "Determining Fabric Yardage," on page 20, plus extra fabric for matching.

* Contrast fabric for welting and banding at "skirt" hem (See **Bias Strip,** on page 102, to calculate fabric yardage.)

* Zipper the height of the chair back (See "Closures," on page 61, for other choices.)

Note: A general guideline for calculating the extra fabric necessitated by matching is to add a repeat for every section that requires centering.

YARDAGE AND CUTTING

1. Review "Blocking: General Guidelines," on page 38. Note that the sequence of blocking a patterned slipcover will differ from the sequence described in this section. (Letters after the section names refer to the chair illustration, on page 37.)

2. Plan motif placement when calculating yardage requirements. Large designs, stripes, and plaids should be centered on all front and back sections, the side of each arm, and on each cushion. Although this slipcover's waterfall style does not call for a separate skirt, any style skirt could be added; mark a skirtline on the chair and plan appropriate yardage for the skirt style chosen.

3. Inside Back (A). The inside chair back from the top edge to the top of the deck. To be sure that your pattern is centered on the inside back once the cushion is in place, put the cushion in the chair before blocking the inside back. Center the pattern carefully between the top of the chair and the top of the cushion, centering the motifs a little more than halfway up from the center point. Pin in darts to make the fabric fit the roll of the back (see **Dart,** on page 105). Now remove the cushion and extend the fabric down to the deck top. *Note:* If slipcovering a wide piece of furniture (such as a sofa), in which case sections need to be joined to create sufficient width, sections should be cut from identical areas of the pattern.

4. Back Cushion Cover, Front and Back, and Boxing. The area on the front and back of the loose back cushion and the band around the cushion depth that includes a zipper for access to the cushion. Place both the seat and back cushion on the chair. Center the pattern carefully between the top of the seat cushion and the top of the back cushion, centering the motifs a little more than halfway up from the center point. *Note:* For multiple cushions, cut all the cushion cover fronts, tops and boxing strips from the identical areas of the pattern. To create the cushion boxing, cut one strip long enough to cover the bottom boxing of the cushion plus 3½ inches to extend up each side. This is where the zipper will be inserted. The remaining boxing strip extends across the cushion top and joins the bottom boxing on the sides. To complete the zipper strip, unpin the bottom boxing strip and use it as a pattern to cut a second zipper strip. Fold one strip in half lengthwise and press. *Note:* You may need to piece the long cushion boxing band. Before cutting any pieces, position the piece for the top of the boxing; it needs to flow from or complement the back cushion.

Assuming that your pattern is directional, the cushion will not be reversible, because reversal would orient the design on the boxing in the wrong direction. In this circumstance, it is not important for the back of the back cushion cover to be identical to the front.

5. Cushion Cover (top and bottom [J] and boxing [K]). The area on the top and bottom of the cushion and the zippered band around the cushion depth. With a patterned fabric, you will want the pattern on the cushion to flow from the inside back and/or the loose back cushion. Place the cushions back on the chair and move the pattern around on the seat cushion top until you find a pleasing arrangement that repeats or complements the pattern on the inside back–back cushion. Cut the top piece slightly larger than cushion size. To block the boxing strip, see Step 4 in Yardage and Cutting.

6. Top Boxing (B). This chair does not have a top boxing piece. If your furniture has top boxing, plan the pattern to match or complement the inside back.

7. Inside Arm (C). The area along the inside arm, up over the top of the arm, to the outside arm seamline (on round-arm furniture only). The pattern should be centered on the arm front to back and between the top of the arm and the top of the cushion. To block this section, place the cushion in the chair and position the fabric appropriately; remove the cushion and extend the fabric down to the deck top. Along the top edge of this arm, use darts to fit the roll of the arm (see **Dart,** on page 105). Allow for tuck-in at the crevice between the inside arm and deck and, if your chair affords it, the inside arm and back. Cut one for each side. *Note:* The seam that joins the inside arm to the outside arm should follow the seam on the upholstery or, on curled or rolled arms without a seam, the slipcover arm seam should fall at the thickest part of the arm. To determine this seam position, refer to "Blocking: General Guidelines," on page 38.

8. Outside Arm (D). The area along the outside of the arm, beginning at a seamline along the length of the arm, to the floor (or to the skirtline on a skirted style). With a T-shaped cushion and a waterfall style, the outside arm piece has two sections. The largest one begins at the back edge and stops in line with the front edge of the arm. The second piece, which extends to the front of the chair and up over the "T" of the deck, will complete the outside arm panel. The pattern, if possible, should match at the seam between the two outside arm sections, with the entire piece centered along the outside arm. Allow 6 to 8 inches of fabric over the deck, 4 inches of fabric on the sides for tuck-in at the deck and seams, and 2 inches below the marked bottom. Cut one for each side.

9. Front Apron (F). The area extending across the chair front width from the deck down to the floor (or skirtline). With the waterfall style, the front apron extends 6 to 8 inches up into the deck and forms a miter at the corner where it meets an outside arm. *Note:* The seam at the corner probably will not have a pattern match. Position the front apron piece so that the pattern flows with the inside back and cushions. Allow 2 inches of fabric below the marked bottom, for adjustment.

10. Deck (G). The area extending from the front apron, upper edge, to the chair back. With the T-shaped deck and the waterfall style, the deck piece does not come all the way out to the front edge of the chair; it stops at the front of the arm where it attaches to the front apron. Allow for tuck-ins along the sides and back. This piece does not need to match anything—it will never show!

11. Shoulder (I). The depth of the seat back extending from the arm upward to the top back. From the remaining smaller pieces, cut one back for each side, allowing as much as 4 inches all around to adjust placement.

12. Front Arm (H). Although this chair has an English arm, which does not include a front, you can see this section on the chair shown on page 37. The front arm extends from the upper arm down to the deck. For that chair, choose a section of the pattern that will be attractive on both sides of the chair, since these two pieces will be mirror images. Avoid placing large motifs here—they can look like headlights and detract from the overall piece. Cut one front arm for each side, allowing as much as 4 inches all around for adjusting placement and turning back side hems.

13. Outside Back (E). The area covering the entire back of the chair down to the floor (or skirtline). If your chair will sit where the back will be visible, plan to cut this section after cutting the inside back and cushion; center the pattern in the area. Otherwise, centered pattern placement on this section is not critical. Also consider your closure choice. Allow 4 inches on the sides for turning back side hems.

14. If a skirt will replace the waterfall style, center the pattern to coordinate with the other front sections. For more skirt information, see "Skirts," on page 56.

SEWING INSTRUCTIONS

1. Pin-fit the slipcover as outlined in "Pin-Fitting: General Guidelines," on page 43, while following the blocking sequence process cited in Yardage and Cutting.

2. Review "Basic Construction," on page 48. The list that follows incorporates those guidelines but makes some changes to conform to this chair.

3. Sew the unwelted seams first. These usually include the tuck-ins around the three sides of the deck and the inside arm–inside back seams. Sew the front apron to the deck.

4. Sew the darts at the upper edge of the inside back panel (see **Dart,** on page 105). Apply welting to the inside back panel on each side, from where the side of the panel meets the arm up to where it meets the outside back (see **Welting,** on page 108).

5. Sew the darts in the inside arm panel and seam the two sections of the outside arm panel. Apply welting to the upper edge of each outside arm panel, from the back edge down to where it meets the deck. Sew each inside arm panel to the outside arm panel, and then attach the shoulder panel, lower edge, to the back edge of the outside arm panels and to the side edge of the inside back.

6. Form a mitered seam at the front corner area, where the front apron–deck panel meets the small section of the outside arm (see **Mitering,** on page 106). There should be excess fabric there for a tuck-in where arm and deck meet.

7. Apply welting around the back edge of the partially constructed slipcover, starting and stopping at the level of the deck. Then sew the outside back panel to the rest of the slipcover, leaving the closure seam unsewn except for 2 inches at the top.

8. Try the slipcover on the chair again. Turn up the excess fabric at the floor so that the fabric fold lies on the floor or just slightly above it. Remove the cover, press in the foldline, and then cut off the excess fabric along the creased line. Cut bias strips 2¼ inches wide for a ½-inch finished binding. Bind the cut edges as instructed in **Binding,** on page 104. *Note:* For a skirt, see "Creating and Attaching the Skirt," on page 48.

9. To insert zipper in back opening, follow the instructions in "Inserting the Zipper Closure," on page 50.

10. To sew the cushion covers, follow the instructions in "Sewing the Cushion Cover," on page 51.

OTTOMAN WITH GATHERED SKIRT

Brush fringe, used instead of welting, adds a new dimension to an ottoman cover. The hem is embellished with a cord with lip, adding weight to the bottom edge. To secure the cover in place, you may attach twill tape ties inside at each corner of the boxing to tie around the ottoman legs.

MATERIALS

* 4½ yards fabric (This amount should suffice for a standard ottoman, up to 22 × 22 inches, with a gathered skirt.)
* Brush fringe trim for welting (If the brush fringe is not full, consider using it in a double layer.)
* ⅜-inch-wide cord on lip for hem trim

YARDAGE AND CUTTING

1. Review "Blocking: General Guidelines," on page 38. If covering an ottoman to match another piece of furniture and working with a patterned fabric, consider centering the same motif on both pieces.

2. Place a piece of fabric across the top of the ottoman. Mark a point 2 inches out from each side and trim off extra fabric. With a patterned fabric, allow up to 4 inches to allow for adjustments.

3. Prepare the boxing strips: Cut four strips of fabric the depth of the upholstery boxing plus 4 inches by the length of each of the four sides plus 4 inches. With patterned fabric, consider motif placement and/or matching this boxing to that on another piece of furniture. Align the boxing strips with the top piece along each corresponding side of the ottoman.

4. To determine the depth of the skirt piece, measure on the ottoman the distance from the bottom of the boxing to the floor; add 1 inch for seam allowance. *Note:* The cord with lip adds the extra length needed for gathering take-up; consider adding ¼ inch to the length for other types of hem treatments. To determine the length of the skirt piece, measure around all four sides of the ottoman and multiply that total by 2½. To determine the number of fabric widths needed for that length, divide that larger total by the fabric width. With patterned fabric, each strip must be cut from the identical part of the pattern.

5. For the hem facing, cut the same number of strips as for the skirt. Each strip should be 3 inches wide.

SEWING INSTRUCTIONS

1. Pin-fit the pieces to the ottoman after reviewing "Pin-Fitting: General Guidelines," on page 43, and following the blocking sequence cited in Yardage and Cutting.

2. Apply brush fringe to the two short edges of two boxing strips on opposite sides of the ottoman. Sew the other two boxing strips to these, making a circle.

3. Apply brush fringe around all four sides of the top piece. Sew the boxing strip to the top piece, matching the corners of the boxing to the corner of the top.

4. Apply brush fringe around the bottom edge of the boxing strip.

5. Seam the facing sections of the skirt and hem, making a circle of each. Divide and mark the skirt strip into quarters.

6. Apply the cord with lip to the hem edge of the skirt piece. Face this edge with the facing strip. Turn under ½ inch on the raw edge of the facing strip. Blindstitch the hem facing into place.

7. Gather the skirt to the finished skirt length (see **Gathering,** on page 106).

8. With right sides together, pin the skirt to the ottoman, matching the marks to the ottoman corners. Distribute the fullness evenly on each side, allowing some extra fullness in the corners.

QUEEN ANNE CHAIR

Soften the look of classic wood side chairs with simple slipcovers that are uniquely detailed.
Double-face satin ribbon is pleated as a welting substitute and pearl buttons create the decorative
and functional back closure. (See page 63 for a detail.)

YARDAGE AND CUTTING

1. The amount of fabric will vary with its width and the directional nature of the fabric and the need to center a pattern. If using a solid color or allover pattern in 54-inch-wide fabric, you will need 1½ yards. When using a narrower or directional fabric, the front-side skirt piece has to be adjusted by splitting it at the front corners and adding seam allowance to those cutlines. To determine actual yardage required for your cover, prepare the pattern pieces as instructed and do a sample layout.

2. Make a template of the chair back and chair seat (see **Template,** on page 108). Make a muslin, making adjustments if needed.

3. Plan the layout once the pattern pieces are prepared. On a solid 54-inch-wide fabric, the front of the chair back and the seat can be placed across a width, with the back pieces across another width. The skirt pieces can then be layed out vertically along the sides parallel to the selvage. When the skirt pieces must be cut horizontally, cut the skirt front and one side from one width and the other side and the skirt back pieces from a second width.

4. Cut the same pieces from the flannel interlining, except that the skirt pieces are only half width, or 4¼ inches.

MATERIALS

* 1½ yards of 54-inch-wide nondirectional fabric (For 48-inch-wide or directional fabric, see Yardage and Cutting details.)

* Flannel interlining, same width and amount as face fabric (A regular lining fabric can be used, but flannel gives the cover body and softness.)

* Double-face satin ribbon (⅞ inch) to be pleated for welting (The pictured slipcover took 12 yards of ribbon that was pleated down to 4 yards.)

* Six 1-inch buttons

SEWING INSTRUCTIONS

1. Pin (and baste, if it makes you more comfortable) the flannel interlining to the wrong side of each corresponding section so that, in the sewing process, they can be treated as one piece. On the skirt pieces pin the interlining to one side, between the foldline and the raw edge.

2. To use your sewing machine to pleat up the ribbon: Place the edge of the ribbon against the right edge of the presser foot (this placement will result in a stitch line ¼ inch from the ribbon edge). Use a thin metal or plastic ruler, such as a 6-inch sewing gauge, to push up ¾ inch of ribbon into

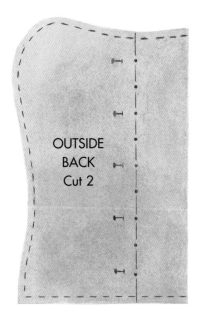

OUTSIDE
BACK
Cut 2

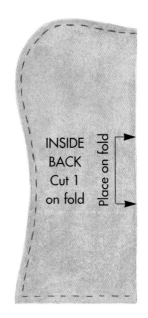

INSIDE
BACK
Cut 1
on fold

Place on fold

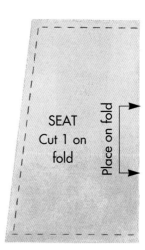

SEAT
Cut 1 on
fold

Place on fold

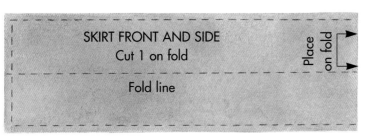

SKIRT FRONT AND SIDE
Cut 1 on fold

Fold line

Place on fold

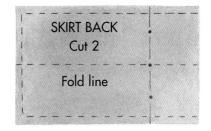

SKIRT BACK
Cut 2

Fold line

a pleat. Stitch the pleat into place. As the needle approaches the end of the pleat, make another. Continue until you have the length of "welting" you need.

3. To prepare the back sections: Press in the foldlines on both pieces; trim away the interlining in the facing to the foldline. Pin the facing into place against the interlining on both pieces; sew it by hand. Make buttonholes in the lefthand side section. Lay the left-side piece over the right one and adjust the overlap so that they match the chair back's front pattern. Mark the overlap position and the button placement; sew on the buttons and repin the sections together.

4. Apply the pleated ribbon trim around the sides and top of the chair back's front piece, ¼ inch from the raw edge; the stitching line made to hold the pleats in place aligns with the stitching line for the cover (allow ½ inch for seam). With right sides together, sew the front and back pieces together along the welted edges.

5. Sew the back edge of the seat piece to the bottom of the chair back's front section.

6. Apply the pleated ribbon trim to the lower edge of the cover, starting at the folded edge of the back opening, across half the back, around the sides and front of the skirt, across the other half back to the folded edge. At the folded edge, allow 1 inch or more of trim to fold back to the inside of the cover.

7. Seam the skirt pieces as needed to go around the cover. Trim away any interlining in the seam allowances and in the facing areas. Press in half along the foldline, and baste the raw edges together. If you are concerned that the interlining may shift later, use some dots of no-sew glue or a narrow strip of fusible web to attach the interlining near the lower edge to the inside half of the skirt piece (the facing side).

8. With right sides together, sew the skirt to the cover, matching foldlines at the back opening and seams or marked circles to the corners. Press seam allowances toward the back; the facing on the skirt is not folded back yet. Press the seam allowances toward the skirt.

9. Fold back the skirt facing and tack into place along the three loose edges. Make the buttonhole and attach the button on the appropriate side.

VANITY STOOL

What could be more practical for a vanity stool than washable terry toweling?
Purchase an extra bath sheet or towels to use as yardage so that your stool will
match your towels and washcloths and can be laundered just as easily.

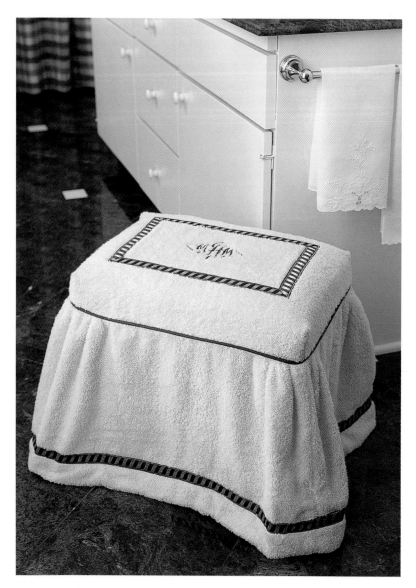

YARDAGE AND CUTTING

1. Prepare pattern pieces based on the size of the stool, and lay them out to determine accurate yardage. Towels are an alternative to cut yardage; use two or three, depending on their size.

2. Terry cloth has a tendency to stretch and shift. To stabilize it, line terry cloth with a stable fabric such as broadcloth or sheeting.

3. To create the pattern for the top piece: Measure the top in both directions, starting and stopping where the legs meet the top or from where you want the skirt to start. Draw a rectangle using those measurements; add ½-inch seam allowance all around. On each side of the rectangle, use a circle mark to note the exact width and length of the stool.

4. To determine the height of the skirt, measure from the point where the top will start to the floor; add ½ inch to the top for seam allowance and 2 inches to the bottom for hem allowance. The skirt width is the distance around the stool plus 5 extra inches in each corner and ½ inch for seam allowance on each edge to be seamed. Mark on the top edge of the skirt the areas to be gathered.

SEWING INSTRUCTIONS

1. To box the corners on the cover top, fold each corner so that a circle from the A side matches up with the adjoining circle from the B side. From the circles out to the folded edge, draw a line perpendicular to the raw edge; stitch along that line. Trim away extra fabric in the triangle, leaving a ½-inch seam allowance.

2. Make welting from ribbon or contrast fabric (see **Welting,** on page 108). Apply around the edge of the top.

MATERIALS

* Approximately 2 yards fabric or towels (Quantity depends on size of stool.)
* Ribbon trim for top and skirt
* Ribbon (1½ inch) for welting (or use contrast fabric)
* Welting cord (⁵⁄₃₂ inch), enough to reach around the stool plus several inches
* Optional: lining

3. Seam together the skirt sections to make a circle. Gather the marked areas.

4. With right sides together, pin and sew the skirt to the top piece, matching the corners of the top to the squares on the skirt. Gathered areas of the skirt come 2½ inches out from each side of the boxed corners on the top piece.

5. Turn up the hem allowance. Place the cover over the stool to check the length and adjust if needed. Sew hem.

6. Apply the ribbon band trim around the bottom of the skirt.

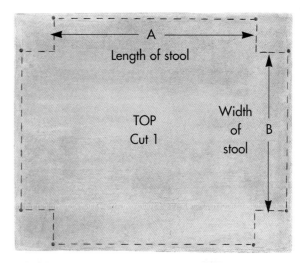

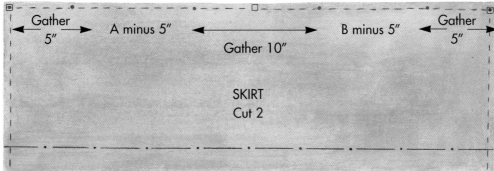

Mitering Flat Trims

Ribbons, braids, and other flat trims with two finished edges often are used to create borders on flat treatments such as Roman shades—and that can require turning corners. The best way to do this is to miter the corner, which means you'll need a little extra trim (an amount equal to the trim width for each corner). Always begin by marking the trim placement lines as noted earlier. The following instructions are for trims with two straight edges; for trims with one straight and one decorative edge, position the straight edge on the placement line and edgestitch only that edge.

1. Position the outer trim edge along the placement line and edgestitch each edge up to 2 inches from the placement line corner intersection.

2. Fold the trim back onto itself at the placement line corner and draw a 45-degree angle from the outer corner to the inner corner; pin along the angle.

3. Fold down the trim to check the angle (the trim should align with the adjacent placement line). Lift the trim back up, remove the pin(s), and stitch the diagonal line.

4. If the trim is bulky, trim the corner close to the stitching.

5. Reposition the trim edge on the adjacent line and continue stitching the trim on the line.

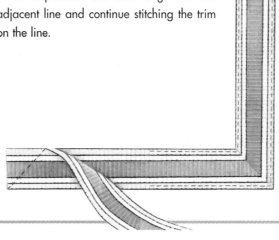

PARSONS CHAIR

Since dining chairs are most often seen from the back, special attention was paid to the closure here. Grosgrain ribbon was used not only for the decorative bows and bottom band trim but also for covering the welting cord.

MATERIALS

* 3½ yards fabric
* Optional: 2 yards lining (Lining at least the skirt is recommended.)
* Optional: 4½ yards grosgrain ribbon (1½ inch) for welting (or use welting cord)
* 7 yards ribbon (⅞ inch) for hem trim and ties
* 4½ yards welting cord (5/32 inch)

YARDAGE AND CUTTING

The instructions that follow are for a lined skirt. If you are not lining the skirt, add 2 inches to the cut depth for a turned-up hem; add yardage if needed.

1. See "Slipcover Basics," on page 36.

2. Enlarge and cut out pattern pieces with front and back side by side, the pleat and seat side by side, and the skirt pieces railroaded side by side (see **Railroading,** on page 107). *Note:* If you are using a directional fabric, you may need to cut the skirt horizontally instead of vertically. The skirt front and sides piece will then need to be seamed. Seam at the corners. Pleats can be added if desired; allow 12 inches for each pleat.

3. For the ribbon ties, cut six 20-inch-long pieces.

SEWING INSTRUCTIONS
Front, Back, and Seat

1. Reinforce and clip all pieces at circles and squares marked "CLIP."

2. Pin ribbon ties to marked locations on each side of the center back seam. Pin and sew pleat piece to each side center back seam. Press seams open. Fold back piece in half, aligning the seams; baste through the center of the seam. Press pleat and pin.

3. Make and apply welting to upper and side edge of back. Clip seam allowance of welting at square.

4. To make dart seams at front corners of the seat: With right sides together, bring the broken lines together. Stitch along the broken lines from raw edge to the point. Trim the dart to a ½-inch seam allowance; press open.

5. With right sides together, pin the lower edge of the front to the back edge of the seat, matching circles. Sew between the circles.

6. With right sides together, pin back to front and seat along side and upper edges, matching circles and squares and opening out clips. Stitch around piece.

7. Apply remaining welting to lower edge of the back and seat.

Skirt

1. Cut lining pieces for the skirt the same size as the face pieces. With right sides together, pin and sew face and lining along the bottom edges. Press seam open and then fold along the seamed edge and press again. Baste side and top edges together.

2. To make the center pleat in the skirt back: With right sides together, fold the piece in half. Mark the pleat 6 inches

out from the foldline and stitch along that line with a basting stitch. Press the pleat flat, aligning the center of the pleat with the basting line.

3. Pin and then sew the side edges of the skirt front and sides to the skirt back. Do not press open the seams.

4. Pin the skirt to the upper section of the chair cover, matching corners, center fronts, and center backs. *Note:* Keep in mind the fact that the back corners of the chair cover are not at the seam, but rather on the back section.

5. At each of the back corners, arrange the extra fabric into pleats with 3 inches of folded fabric at each side. The seam should fall at a pleat foldline.

6. Apply ribbon trim to the bottom edge of the skirt, 1 inch up from the folded edge. The raw ends can be treated with a seam sealant or glue and hidden in a pleat fold.

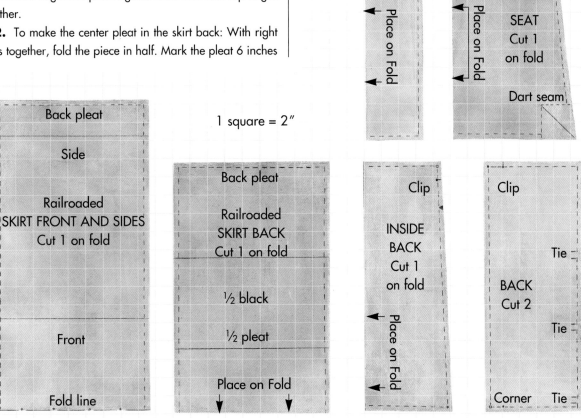

1 square = 2″

TIE-ON CUSHION

Add comfort and style to stools and chairs with easy-to-make one-piece cushions.
Grosgrain ribbon threads through grommets and around the legs to hold the covers in place.

MATERIALS
* 1 yard fabric
* 1 yard lining fabric
* 6½ yards ribbon (⅝ inch)
* Eight ¼-inch inside diameter grommets
* Fiberfill

YARDAGE AND CUTTING

1. Make a template of your chair seat (see **Template,** on page 108). Add ¼ inch all around the template.

2. Trace the template onto another piece of paper or fabric that is larger all around by at least 7 inches. Add 6 inches to all four side edges, but not to the back support cutouts. At the lower edge of the four back corners, measure out 1 inch and redraw the side edge of the flap from that point up to the template line. Add ½-inch seam allowance all around the new template, including the back support cutouts.

3. Cut out this pattern from the face fabric.

4. Cut out the lining pieces from the lining fabric.

SEWING INSTRUCTIONS

1. With right sides together, stitch lining pieces together along center seam, leaving space between dots open for turning. Press seam open.

2. With right sides together, pin and then sew the face and lining fabrics. Press the seams open. Through the opening in the lining, turn the piece right side out.

3. On the lining side of the cover, appropriately position the first template you made and draw around it. Stitch around the cover on those lines.

4. Apply the ribbon around the seat cover at the bottom seamed edges only, mitering the trim at the front corners.

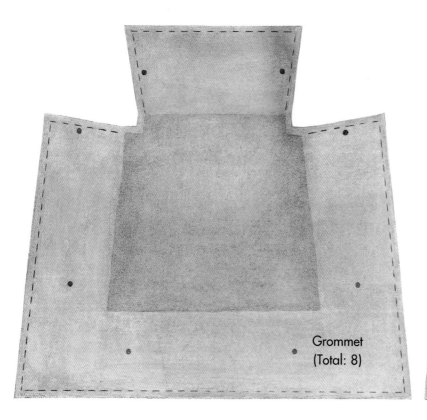

Grommet
(Total: 8)

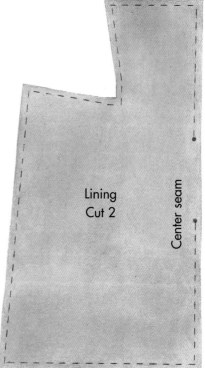

Lining
Cut 2

Center seam

5. On the lining side, mark the positions for the grommets. For most chairs, the grommets will be 3 inches up from the hem edge and 2 inches in from the corner of the first template. Before inserting the grommets put the cover on the chair; the grommets should fall just below the chair's apron and just inside the chair legs. Make adjustments if needed, and then insert grommets.

6. Through the opening in the lining, lightly stuff the chair seat with fiberfill. Slipstitch the opening by hand.

7. Place the cover on the chair. Cut the remaining ribbon into four pieces. At each corner, thread the ribbon from front to back through one grommet, bring the end around the back of the chair leg, and take it back to the front through the other grommet. Tie ends in a bow and trim ribbon as desired.

FOLDING CHAIR

The ubiquitous folding chair is all dressed up in glazed chintz. A coordinating miniplaid print,
cut on the bias, bands the skirt hem, welts the seat and back seam,
and edges the bouffant bow. (See page 5 for a detail.)

YARDAGE AND CUTTING

1. Enlarge the pattern pieces and make a muslin (refer to "Making the Projects in This Section," on page 66). Make adjustments if needed, then cut pattern pieces from cover fabric.

2. Mark and reinforce all corner and clip areas (see **Reinforcing,** on page 107). Mark and number the notches.

3. From the contrast fabric, cut and make welting (see **Welting,** on page 108). For the bound hem, cut enough additional strips, 2½ inches wide, to make 3½ yards of bias strips (see **Bias Strip,** on page 102).

4. Cut the ties, 43 inches long × 8 inches wide, shaping the ends as shown on the tie pattern.

SEWING INSTRUCTIONS

1. Make dart seam (see **Dart,** page 105) in seat and inside back section, matching circles and #1 notches. Apply welting around this piece.

MATERIALS

* 3 yards fabric for chair cover
* 1 yard contrast fabric for welting and binding hem
* Optional: Companion fabric for appliquéing hem area
* 7½ yards welting cord

2. Baste pleat in back section.

3. Make the ties. Apply the welting cord around three sides of two ties, leaving the notched side untrimmed. With right sides together, sew the other tie pieces to the welted ones on the welted edges only. Turn right side out; press. Pull out and cut off 1 inch of welting cord at ends of ties. Pin ties to front-side skirt piece, matching circles and #5 notches.

4. Sew the front-side skirt to the back–back skirt, right sides together and matching #2 notches. On the front-side skirt, gather the section between the circles to 5 inches.

5. Pin the seat–inside back to the skirt section put together in Step 4, matching notches #3 and #4 and center fronts and back. Clip seam allowances as needed. Gathers should fall at the front corners on the seat and cover 2½ inches on either side of the #4 notches.

6. Put cover over folding chair and pin up hem; press into place.

7. Three styling options for the hem area can be used alone or in combination. The instructions for each option follow.

• **Traditional Hem.** Sew turned-up hem.

• **Bound Hem.** Cut off the hem allowance and bind (see **Binding,** on page 104).

• **Appliqué.** Prepare the companion fabric as described in **Appliqué,** on page 102. Cut out the desired motifs and pin them along the hem edge. Fuse into place. Cut off turned-up hem allowance. Bind edge (see **Binding,** on page 104).

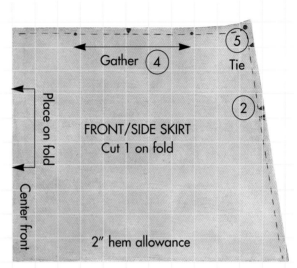

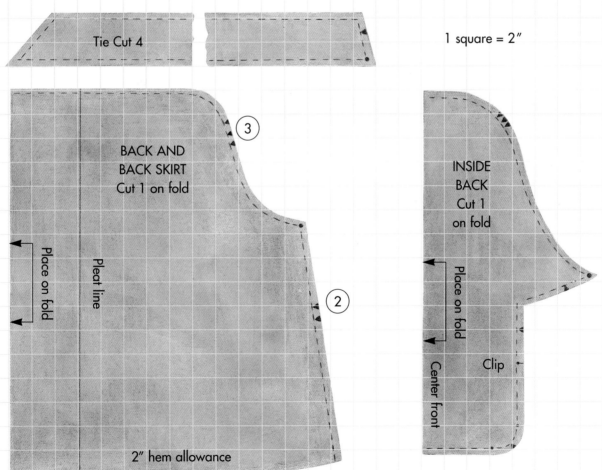

1 square = 2"

SOFA WITH WATERFALL SKIRT

You can simplify the lines of a sofa by replacing an attached skirt with a waterfall skirt that falls from the platform and outside arm seam and is an extension of the front arm panel. Band trim at the skirt edge adds weight and protects the fabric from shoe marks.

MATERIALS

* Fabric as calculated for a tailored skirt in "Determining Fabric Yardage," on page 20.

* ⅜-inch cord with lip, for welting

* Zipper the height of the sofa back (See "Closures," on page 61, for other choices.)

* 1½-inch-wide band trim the length of the distance around the sofa or skirt plus 6 inches for ease and end finish

YARDAGE AND CUTTING

1. Review "Blocking: General Guidelines," on page 38. *Note:* If using a napped fabric, such as velvet or corduroy, be sure to cut all the pieces with the nap in the same direction. (The letter after each section name refers to the chair illustration on page 37.)

2. Inside Back (A). The inside sofa back from the top edge to the top of the deck. Follow the three-cushion design of the upholstery and cut three separate sections. Allow enough extra fabric for tuck-in where the inside back meets the inside arm. With sofas having deep grooves running vertically between the back pillow sections, ignore the crevices, because keeping fabric tucked into these grooves is difficult; accent the sections by applying welting in the vertical seams (see **Welting,** on page 108).

3. Top Boxing (B). The top of the sofa back; on this sofa, running down both sides to the outside arm seam. Plan sections and seams to correspond to the sections of the inside back. Allow 3 inches all around for minor adjustments.

4. Inside Arm (C). The area along the inside arm, up over the top of the arm, to the outside arm seamline. Allow for tuck-in at the crevice between the inside arm and the deck and, if your sofa will allow it, the inside arm and the back. Cut one for each side. *Note:* The seam that joins the inside arm to the outside arm should follow the seam on the upholstery. Or, on curved or rolled arms without a seam, the slipcover arm seam should fall at the thickest part of the arm. To determine this seam position, refer to "Blocking: General Guidelines," on page 38.

5. Outside Arm (D). The area along the outside of the arm beginning at a seamline along the length of the arm, to the floor. Allow 2 inches beyond the floorline. Cut one for each side.

6. Front Apron (F). The area extending across the sofa front width up onto the deck down to the floorline. Divide the front apron into three sections to correspond to the sections on the inside back. Allow 2 inches beyond the floorline.

7. Deck (G). The area extending from the front edge to the sofa back; the front edge of the deck will actually be an extension of the front apron. Allow for tuck-in along the sides and back. Seaming can be anywhere needed, because the deck is not visible on the finished slipcover.

8. Front Arm (H). The area at the front of the arm extending from the upper arm down to the floor. From remaining small pieces, cut one for each side, allowing as much as 4 inches all around for adjusting placement.

9. Outside Back (E). The area covering the entire back of the sofa down to the floor. Any seams should follow the sections on the top boxing and inside back; allocate one of the interior (not corner) seams for the zipper. (See photo on page 61.) *Note:* If the sofa will be against a wall, the outside back can be in two sections instead of three, with the closure in the center seam. Allow 2 inches below the floorline.

10. Cushion Covers, Top and Bottom (J), and Boxing (K). The area on the top and bottom of the cushion and the zippered band around the cushion depth. For the cushion cover top and bottom, measure the cushion top length and width and cut two identical panels slightly larger than those measurements, being careful that the lengthwise grain runs from the cushion back to front. To create the cushion boxing, cut three bands: two the length of the cushion back edge plus 7 inches by half the cushion depth plus 1 inch, and one the cushion perimeter measurement minus the other bands' length measurement plus 7 inches by the cushion depth plus 1 inch. Piece boxing bands as needed. Make three cushions.

SEWING INSTRUCTIONS

1. Pin-fit the slipcover as outlined in "Pin-Fitting: General Guidelines," on page 43, while following the blocking sequence cited in Yardage and Cutting.

2. Review "Basic Construction," on page 48. The list that follows incorporates those guidelines but makes some changes to conform to this sofa.

3. Sew the tuck-ins around the three sides of the deck and the inside arm–inside back seams.

4. Sew the front apron sections together without welting. Sew the joined sections to the deck panel.

5. Apply welting to each vertical side of the center inside back section (see **Welting,** on page 108). Sew the outside sections to the center one.

6. Apply welting to each vertical side of the center top boxing section. Sew the two outside sections of the boxing strip to the center one. Apply welting to the long side of the boxing strip that will attach to the inside back. Sew the boxing strip to the top edge of the inside back, matching the seams on the two pieces.

7. Apply welting to the curved area of the inside back, where the inside back meets the inside arm, stopping the welting 8 inches above the deck; that 8-inch section should have enough fabric for tuck-in.

8. Apply welting to the upper edge of each outside arm panel, then sew each inside arm panel to the outside arm panel. Sew outside arm–inside arm panel to the inside back, allowing for tuck-in below the welting.

9. Apply welting to the front edge of each inside-outside arm section, starting at the deck level on the inside and stopping at the same level on the outside (corner) edge. Then sew each front arm panel to the inside-outside arm section and front apron panel.

10. Apply welting around the back edge of the partially constructed slipcover, starting and stopping the welting at the point, on each side of the sofa, that is at the level of the deck.

11. Sew together the sections of the outside back as planned, leaving one seam open to within 2 inches of the top. Then sew the outside back panel to the rest of the slipcover.

12. Try the slipcover on the sofa again and turn up the excess fabric at the floor to the *right* side so that the fabric lies on the floor or just slightly above it. Remove the cover, press in the foldline, and then trim the hem fabric to 1 inch. Pin hem. Sew the band trim to the hem edge, starting and stopping at the closure opening. *Note:* For a skirted finish, see "Creating and Attaching the Skirt," on page 48.

13. To insert zipper in back opening, follow the instructions in "Inserting the Zipper Closure," on page 50.

14. To sew the cushion covers, follow the instructions in "Sewing the Cushion Cover," on page 51.

DIRECTOR'S CHAIR

Add a separate cushion and a bold appliqué design to a director's chair cover for comfort and individual style.
New fusible adhesives make the appliqué process fast, easy, and foolproof.

MATERIALS

* 4 yards of 44- to 45-inch fabric or 3½ yards 54-inch fabric, solid or allover pattern
* Contrast fabric for appliqué and buttons
* Fusible web
* Two ¼-inch self-cover buttons
* Polyester fiberfill for cushion

YARDAGE AND CUTTING

1. See "Slipcover Basics," on page 36.
2. Enlarge pattern pieces and make a muslin (refer to "Making the Projects in This Section," on page 66). Make adjustments if needed, then cut pattern pieces from cover fabric. For the cushion, cut a rectangle 21 inches wide × 36 inches long.
3. Mark and reinforce all circles, squares, and clips. Mark and number the notches.

SEWING INSTRUCTIONS
Cover

Letters after the section names refer to labels on the accompanying grid.

1. On each arm and skirt piece (A), make a dart seam where indicated. Fold on the foldline, keeping right sides, seamlines, and squares together. Stitch along the seamline between the small circle and the square, backstitching at each end to reinforce. Press seam open.

2. Pin one arm and skirt piece (A) to each side of the seat and skirt piece (B), keeping right sides together and matching circles and #1 notches. Open the clipped corner. Stitch seams, stopping at the large circle.

3. With right sides together, sew center back seam of back and skirt pieces (D), matching #9 notches.

4. With right sides together, pin inside back (C) and back and skirt (D), matching #2 notches. Stitch between small circles. Continue pinning around the corner and down the sides, matching large and small circles and #3 notches, opening out clips as needed. Stitch between circles, around the corner, and down to the squares on the sides.

5. With right sides together, pin seat and skirt (B) and inside back (C) along edges with #4 notches. Stitch between the large circles, backstitching to reinforce at each end.

6. Pin inside back (C) and back and skirt (D) to arms and skirt (A), matching #5 notches, small circles, squares, and #6 notches; open out clips as needed. Sew from large circle to the square. Stop stitching. Move the intersecting seam allowance out of the way, and then sew from the square to the bottom of the skirt.

7. On the arm and skirt piece (A) bring #7 notches together; sew from square of the dart seam to the small circle. Pin seat and skirt (B) to arm and skirt (A), matching #8 notches and seam to the small circle.

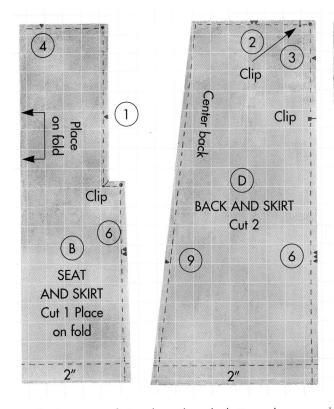

1 square = 2"

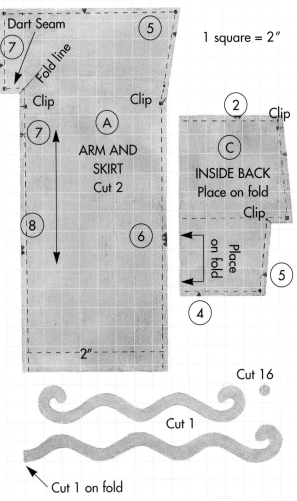

Cut 16

Cut 1

Cut 1 on fold

8. Press up and pin a hem along the bottom edge.

9. Prepare the contrast fabric for appliquéing (see **Appliqué,** on page 102). Position the cutout appliqués above the hem, allowing 1½ inches from the bottommost point on the appliqué to the hemline; iron appliqué into place.

10. Sew the hem.

Cushion

1. With right sides together, fold the cushion rectangle in half so it measures 21 inches wide × 18 inches long. Sew around the three open sides, leaving a 9-inch opening on the longest side for turning and stuffing. Mark the foldline on both sides of the cover.

2. To box the cushion, fold the corner matching seams and marked foldlines. At each of the four corners, draw a line perpendicular to the seam and 1 inch down from the corner. Sew along that line, backstitching to reinforce.

3. Turn the cover right side out. Stuff with fiberfill and slipstitch the opening.

4. Cover buttons with the contrast fabric according to the package directions. Attach them onto the cover 6 inches in from each side seam and halfway between the top and bottom.

BREUER CHAIR

Synthetic suede is ideal for chair covers. It doesn't ravel when cut, has great body, is easy to decorate with cord laced through punched holes, and even goes in the washer and dryer. Use polyester or cotton thread instead of monofilament thread, however, for sewing the cover.

YARDAGE AND CUTTING

1. See "Slipcovers Basics," on page 36. Enlarge the pattern pieces and make a muslin (refer to "Making the Projects in This Section," on page 66).

2. On the accompanying pattern grid, the back section is imposed on the front-seat section because the top portions of both are identical. Make separate pattern pieces.

3. Cut rectangle, for the cushion front, 21½ inches wide × 19 inches long. Cut two other rectangles for the cushion back, each 11¾ inches wide × 19 inches long.

SEWING INSTRUCTIONS
Cover

1. Sew the front-seat to the back, matching #1 notches. Start and stop sewing at the circles. Double-topstitch the seam open by stitching from the right side ³⁄₁₆ inch out on each side of the seam.

2. Sew skirt sections together, matching #2 and #3 notches. Double-topstitch only the front corner seams open.

3. Pin into place the pleats at the back corners.

4. Sew seamed skirt section to the back and front-seat section, matching center fronts and backs.

5. Pin up hem.

6. Use hole punch to make holes in the hem area, ½ inch up from folded hem edge and 1 inch apart. Use the cord to saddlestitch along the hem edge.

7. After the cushion is made, place the cover on the chair and the cushion on the seat. On the seat of the cover, mark the position for the hook side of the Velcro dots. Take cover off and sew dots into place.

MATERIALS
* 3¼ yards fabric
* 10 yards cord
* Hole punch to produce very small holes
* 8- to 9-inch zipper
* Polyester fiberfill for cushion
* 4 Velcro sew-on dots or squares

Note: If you are working with a synthetic suede fabric, remember that pins leave holes. Try to use paper clips or binding and hem clips to hold the fabric layers together.

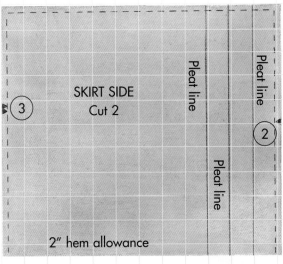

SKIRT SIDE
Cut 2

Pleat line

Pleat line

③

②

Pleat line

2" hem allowance

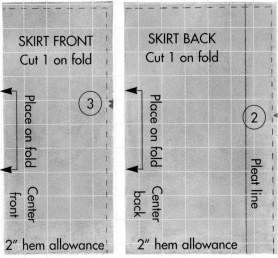

SKIRT FRONT
Cut 1 on fold

Place on fold

Center front

③

2" hem allowance

SKIRT BACK
Cut 1 on fold

Place on fold

Center back

②

Pleat line

2" hem allowance

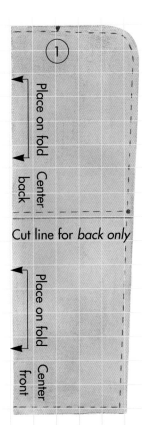

①

Place on fold

Center back

Cut line for *back only*

Place on fold

Center front

BACK AND FRONT
AND SEAT
Cut 1 of each
on fold

1 square = 2"

Cushion

1. To make the back of the cushion, seam the two back sections together with a 1-inch seam along the 19-inch edge, leaving an 8-inch area for zipper insertion. Press open the seam and insert the zipper. Sew the loop side of Velcro dots in all four corners, 3 inches in from each side.

2. With right sides together, sew the cushion front and back pieces together, leaving the zipper open. Turn cover right side out; press. Topstitch close to the outside edge.

3. To make the flange edge for the saddlestitching, stitch around the cover ⅞ inch in from the outside edge.

4. Saddlestitch the cushion by following the cover instructions in Step 6, Sewing Instructions.

5. Through zipper opening, stuff cover with fiberfill. *Note:* A muslin cover can be made to be stuffed with fiberfill and slipstitched closed. The muslin pillow can then be placed through the zipper opening in the cushion cover.

BUTTERFLY CHAIR

The shape of a butterfly chair cover suggests the silhouette of an animal hide. This zebra-print cover is finished just as you would a skin rug, with green felt that has just been pinked on both edges.

MATERIALS

* 1½ yards face fabric
* 1½ yards coordinating fabric for lining
* ¼ yard felt

YARDAGE AND CUTTING

1. See "Slipcover Basics," on page 36.

2. Enlarge the pattern pieces and make a muslin (refer to "Making the Projects in This Section," on page 66). Make adjustments if needed.

3. Cut one seat and one back from each fabric; cut the pockets from the face fabric. If you are using a directional fabric, use chalk to mark the top on each fabric piece.

4. To make the trim strips, cut enough 1-inch-wide strips from the felt to make 4¼ yards. Use pinking shears to trim the edges after straight-cutting them.

SEWING INSTRUCTIONS

1. Face and lining fabrics: With right sides together, pin and sew the seat to the back, along the lower curved edge. Leave a 9-inch section unseamed in the middle of the back piece seam; you will turn this section later. Trim seam to ¼ inch in seamed area only. Press seam open.

2. Hem the straight edge of each pocket. Press under ¾ inch on each pocket and press that hem allowance in half for a double hem. Stitch close to the folded edge. With heavy fabrics, zigzag or serge the raw edges; press up ¾ inch and sew into place.

3. With right sides together, pin pockets to the corresponding corners on the back and seat of the face fabric, matching circles.

4. With right sides together, pin the face and lining, sandwiching the pocket. Sew all around the piece.

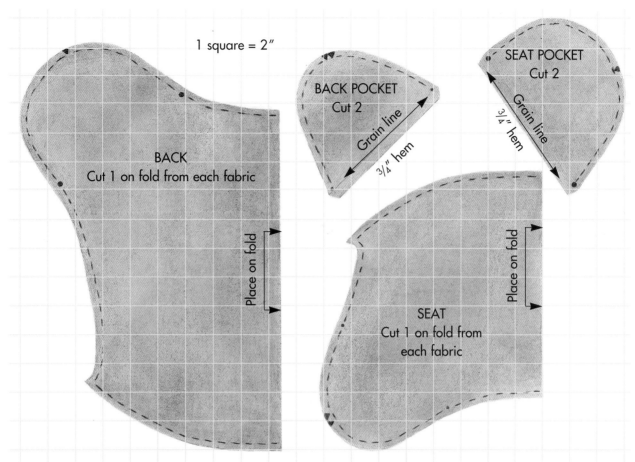

1 square = 2″

BACK POCKET
Cut 2

Grain line

3/4″ hem

SEAT POCKET
Cut 2

Grain line

3/4″ hem

BACK
Cut 1 on fold from each fabric

Place on fold

SEAT
Cut 1 on fold from each fabric

Place on fold

5. Trim seam allowances between pockets to ¼ inch and clip if needed. Leave seam allowance in pocket areas, but notch out the curve to eliminate fullness when the cover is turned right side out.

6. Turn cover through the seam opening; pocket will be on lining side. Press edges and close opening.

7. Topstitch around outside of the cover, ¼ inch in from the edge. Position the cut strips of felt around the cover on the lining side so that the center of the strip aligns with the top-stitched line. Sew the trim to the cover, restitching over the topstitched line, overlapping the felt ends where they meet.

OPTIONAL CONSTRUCTION WITH SINGLE LAYER

1. Purchase wide double-fold bias tape or extra fabric to custom-make bias binding from the cover fabric or contrasting fabric.

2. Follow preceding sewing instructions through Step 2.

3. With wrong sides together, pin pockets to corresponding corners on the back and seat, matching circles.

4. Bind the cover with bias strips (see **Bias Strip,** on page 102).

SKIRTED BUTTERFLY CHAIR

Skirting a butterfly chair changes its form and increases the opportunity to use more fabric.
Mixing a trio of prints separates the undulating curves and accents the trim band and button detail.

MATERIALS

* 2¼ yards fabric for seat, welting, and hem banding (A)
* 2¼ yards fabric for sides (B)
* 1¾ yards fabric for front and back (C)
* 4½ yards welting cord (⁵⁄₃₂ inch)
* Four 1¼-inch self-cover buttons

Notes:

1. If making all pieces from one fabric, use 5 yards total.
2. You will make the pillow from scraps.
3. This cover must be placed over the regular canvas butterfly seat.

YARDAGE AND CUTTING

The letters designating fabric pieces are defined in the materials list.

1. See "Slipcover Basics," on page 36.

2. Enlarge and then cut the pattern pieces from muslin. Make adjustments if needed.

3. From Fabric A cut the seat front and back. Be sure to mark the position of the overlap seam. If you are using a directional fabric, use chalk to mark the top of the pattern pieces.

4. From Fabric A cut 4½ yards of bias strips (see **Bias Strip,** on page 102).

5. From Fabric A cut 4 banding strips, preferably on the bias, 3 inches wide by the hem width of each skirt pattern piece, for a total of 3 yards. If you can take advantage of your fabric's print to create a special banding, be sure you center the pattern on each piece.

6. From Fabric B cut two skirt sides.

7. From Fabric C cut the front and back skirt pieces.

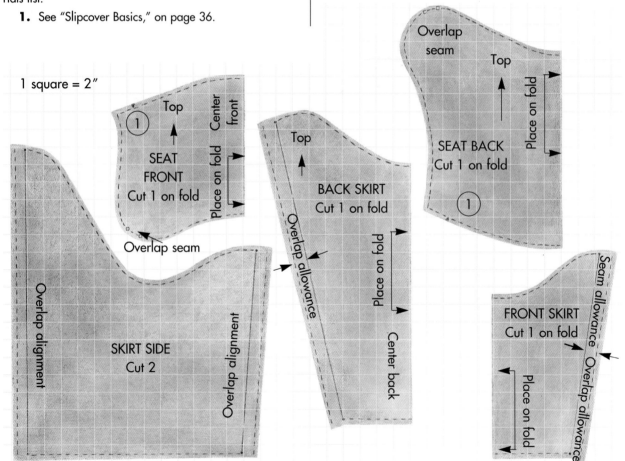

1 square = 2″

SEAT FRONT — Cut 1 on fold

BACK SKIRT — Cut 1 on fold

SEAT BACK — Cut 1 on fold

SKIRT SIDE — Cut 2

FRONT SKIRT — Cut 1 on fold

SEWING INSTRUCTIONS

1. With right sides together, pin and sew the two seat pieces along the lower curved edge. Press seam open. Make and apply welting around the seat section.

2. Apply the banding to the bottom edge of all skirt pieces (see **Banding,** on page 102).

3. On front and back skirt pieces, press under the overlap allowance (1¾ inches). Lay these pieces over the corresponding skirt sides, matching circles and raw edges. Topstitch the skirt sections together, 1½ inches from the folded edge on the front and back skirt pieces.

4. With right sides together, pin the skirt to the seat section, matching center fronts and backs. Position the overlap seam between the marked squares on the seat pieces. Sew all around the piece. Press seamed areas.

LADDERBACK CHAIR

The wooden back slats and rush seat of a ladderback chair can be softened and enhanced by the addition of padded back and seat cushions. Perle cotton, chosen to match the decorative chair ties, is used to create tufts, to add detail, and to control the padding.

MATERIALS

* 4 yards fabric for seat, back cover, and welting
* 4 chair tassels with a 27- to 34-inch spread
* 1¼ yards lining for seat and back cover, in a coordinating color
* 1¼ yards fleece batting for seat and back
* Polyester fiberfill for seat filling
* ½ yard sew-on Velcro fastening for seat back
* 3 colors of perle cotton floss for tufting, 1 skein each color
* Welting cord (⁵⁄₃₂ inch), enough to reach around the seat and around all four sides, one bottom edge, and the top of the back cover.

YARDAGE AND CUTTING

For a fabric 48 inches wide or wider, the suggested yardage should be sufficient for any ladderback chair. If you are concerned about fabric quantity, prepare pattern pieces as instructed in Steps 1 and 2 and do a sample layout.

1. To create the back cover pattern: Cut the paper you are using for the pattern to the width of the back between the upright side supports. Tape the pattern to the back of the chair. Trace the shape of the top and bottom slats across the width of the paper. Trace this shape onto another piece of paper and add ½-inch seam allowance all around. At the bottom of the pattern add a 1½-inch extension for a flap to wrap under the bottom slat, to create a closure.

2. To create the seat pattern: Make a **template** of the seat (see page 108), making sure that it is large enough to allow the skirt to hang straight; add ¾ inch for seam allowance all around the four edges but only ½ inch in the cutout corners. (The extra ¼ inch allows for the fiberfill stuffing.)

3. Plan and cut the skirt: The skirt is in two pieces, one for the front and sides and one for the back; it stops at the edge of the cutouts for the back chair supports. The finished depth of the seat skirt is 4½ inches, requiring a cut depth of 10 inches (4½ inches doubled plus 1 inch for seam allowance). Plan pleats so that they are close to the same size on each side, meet at the corners, and have a half pleat at each end; allow 6 to 10 inches of fabric for each pleat. Add 1 inch at the end of each piece for seam allowance and plan for any seam to fall within a pleat. Where pattern placement in the pleats is important, experiment with uncut fabric against the seat template to determine what works and how much fabric width is needed to achieve the desired look. When you are satisfied, cut the pieces.

4. From the main fabric, lining, and fleece batting: Cut one back cover the full size of the template; cut the second without the 1½-inch extension. Cut one seat the size of the template. Cut out the pieces for the skirt as planned.

5. Cut bias strips for welting from remaining fabric (see **Bias Strip,** on page 102).

SEWING INSTRUCTIONS
Back

1. Pin fleece batting to the wrong side of the back cover pieces.

2. Make welting from bias strips (see **Welting,** on page 108). Apply welting to the top edge of one of the back cover pieces; seam the two back cover pieces together at the top edge only. Pin the center of the welting to hold the cord in place, and then pull out ¾ inch of cord at each end and cut it off so that there is no cord in the seam allowance. Now apply the welting all around the seamed back cover piece, except for the bottom of the piece with the flap extension.

3. Prepare the lining pieces by sewing them together along the top edge. Position the loop side of the Velcro fastener to the right side of the lining section without the flap extension; sew the fastener horizontally across the piece, starting ¾ inch up from the raw edge. With right sides together, pin the lining to the face section. Sew them, leaving a 10-inch opening in the flap extension for turning. Trim away the fleece in the seam allowance to the stitching line, including the side with the opening. Clip the corners. Turn the piece right side out and press.

4. Turn under the seam allowance and pin the opening closed. Sew the hook side of the Velcro fastener across the right side of the flap extension.

5. Attach a tassel to each end of the top seam on the cover.

6. Make and attach the tufts: Each tuft contains two loop pieces that are tied together. For each loop, cut 1 strand of embroidery floss in each color, each 28 inches long. Hold the strands together and wrap them around a 1½-inch piece of cardboard to create seven loops; slip loops off the cardboard. Place one loop atop the second at a right angle; tie together at the center, using an 8-inch strand of the three colors of floss. Leave the long ends. Thread a needle with one set of long ends and push through the cover at the desired spot; repeat with the second set of ends and push through about ⅛ inch away from the first. Ties ends together securely on the wrong side. Spread out the loops to form a circle.

Seat

1. Pin the fleece batting to the wrong side of the seat piece. Sew the welting around the piece, stopping and starting at the cutouts for the chair back supports.

2. Prepare the skirt: With right sides together, fold each piece in half lengthwise and seam the ends. Clip corner. Turn the fabric right side out and press each strip in half. Baste raw edges together. Pin in pleats as planned for each strip; baste.

3. With right sides together, pin and sew the skirt strips around the seat piece.

4. With right sides together, pin and sew the lining to the seat piece, leaving an opening for turning and stuffing. Trim away fleece in the seam allowance to the stitching line; clip corners. Turn the fabric right side out and press. Lightly fill the seat with fiberfill and close the opening.

5. Attach the chair tassels: Position the center of the tassel cord in the corner of the back supports cutout. Tack the cord along the seam to the outside edge of the seat.

6. Make and attach tufts (see Step 6 of sewing instructions for the back).

Tools, Terms, and Techniques

Part 4 is a handy reference for Parts 1 through 3, offering in-depth information about basic techniques used to construct the slipcovers illustrated in this book, and an overview of the supplies you'll use. Before you begin any slipcover project, be sure you have on hand the following materials and tools and that you are familiar with the terms and techniques that apply to your slipcover. A final tip: As you work, keep your work area tidy.

This will cut down on time wasted looking for that runaway ruler, chalk, or thread snips. An orderly work area also helps eliminate mistakes caused by distraction and minimizes cleanup.

LEFT: *A traditional damask upholstered camelback sofa changes personality with a casual, tough denim striped slipcover.*

SLIPCOVER TOOLS

ADEQUATE, ORGANIZED WORK AREA: For the most satisfying slipcovering experience, have ample room around the furniture being covered and enough space around your sewing machine to allow you to work unhampered. If possible, work in a room where you can leave the sewing machine, ironing board, and worktable set up for the duration of the project.

CALCULATOR, PENCIL, AND PAPER: This trio will help you use the measurement method detailed in Part 1.

CUTTING TOOLS: Make sure you have **sharp dressmaker's shears** at least 7 inches long for cutting out slipcover pieces, plus **small embroidery scissors or thread snips** for clipping threads and seam allowances. To avoid extra work later, clip all thread tails as you work; wearing thread snips on a ribbon or cord around your neck will keep them close at hand. **Pinking shears** can also be helpful for clean-finishing seam allowances on ravel-prone fabrics. Although optional, a **rotary cutter and mat** can be real time-savers when cutting boxing, skirts, and bias strips.

FABRIC GLUE: Use this to patch torn upholstery or, when appropriate, for basting trims into place.

IRON AND IRONING BOARD: Your iron should have steam capabilities for pressing seams and removing wrinkles. Check that your ironing board is structurally sound (slipcovers can be weighty and cumbersome), or consider covering a table with a wool blanket to create a large sturdy pressing area. Avoid pressing on the right side of the slipcover; when you must press on the right side, use a **pressing cloth** to avoid unsightly shine at seams.

MARKING CHALK: Although **tailor's chalk,** also called **dressmaker's chalk** (both available in block or pencil form), is commonly used for marking fabrics, basic **blackboard chalk** makes bolder marks and is easier to brush out. Both are available in a wide range of colors. Air-soluble marker works well on light-colored fabrics.

MEASURING TOOLS: These are vital to your project's success: a 120-inch reinforced **fiberglass tape measure** (avoid cloth tape measures, which tend to stretch and tear), a **metal or plastic T-square** for marking and squaring, a **6-inch see-through ruler or seam gauge** for measuring seam allowances, and a **12-inch ruler** for marking skirtlines.

NEEDLES: For your sewing machine, you'll need a size 14 (90) for lightweight fabrics, size 16 (100) for mediumweight fabrics, or a size 18 (110) or a "jeans needle" for heavyweight fabrics. You may also need a **curved upholstery needle** for diagonally basting batting to channels or crevices or for holding batting to foam.

PINS: You'll need three types: stainless-steel **dressmaker's pins** for pin-fitting, especially at curved seamlines where precision is important; **T-pins** for anchoring fabric to furniture; and extra-long **quilter's pins** with large heads for long simple seams. In addition, you may want to have some **binder clips** (available at stationery stores) or **hair clips** on hand to secure fabrics that should not be pinned, such as synthetic suedes.

SEAM RIPPER: Even an expert sewer makes a mistake now and then. Always rip with care, especially on delicate and lightweight fabrics.

SEWING MACHINE: Any portable, cabinet, or industrial machine that's in good working order and can sew through at least six layers of the desired fabric will do. To avoid overtaxing your machine and your patience, test-sew through multiple layers of swatches of your intended fabric before purchasing yardage.

SEWING MACHINE ATTACHMENTS: A **zipper foot,** adjustable to the left or right of the needle, is necessary for installing zippers; it's also handy for making and applying welting, though you may want to opt for a **welt foot** (designed specifically for this task) if your machine has one. And, if you're adding a gathered skirt to your slipcover, an adjustable **ruffler attachment** can dramatically speed the gathering process.

STAPLE GUN: Use this to attach Velcro fasteners to furniture when appropriate.

TUBE-TURNING TOOL: A notion for turning tubes of fabric right side out. Particularly useful for spaghetti ties or inserting elastic or cord into the tube.

BASIC SLIPCOVER MATERIALS

CLOSURES: Heavy-duty metal zippers (available in a wide range of lengths, from 12 to 72 inches) are the most commonly used closures. However, also consider other utilitarian closures: snap tape; hook-and-loop fastener tape, such as Velcro; and functional decorative closures, such as buttons and ties and lacing through grommets. Determine your closure choice and placement before beginning, so you can purchase a sufficient length or quantity. See Part 2 for details on inserting zippers and using alternative closures. Regardless of the closure used on the slipcover, the cushion covers are usually fastened with zippers. Unless you're changing the cushion style, select a zipper that is the same length as the zipper in the original cushion cover.

FABRIC: See Part 1 for details on choosing appropriate fabrics and determining yardages.

POLYESTER BATTING: Use where needed to pad or even the surface of existing furniture. If necessary, secure the batting by sewing with a curved upholstery needle and thread.

THREAD: Choose cotton or cotton-wrapped polyester thread: heavy-duty for heavy fabrics like sailcloth, corduroy, and denim; regular all-purpose thread for medium- to lightweight fabrics like calico, chambray, and sheeting; and transparent monofilament for making welting.

TRIM: If you plan to apply welting to your slipcover seams, you'll need enough $6/32$- to $1/4$-inch-diameter cotton cording for all planned welted seams, plus extra fabric for cutting bias strips to cover the welting. See Part 1 for details on determining yardages and **Welting,** on page 108, for instructions on making and applying welting. Or choose from the array of trim choices detailed in Part 1.

Use this section as a quick reference to the frequently used slipcover-related terms and techniques in this book.

APPLIQUÉ

Applying one fabric to another as a decorative feature (below). There are a number of appliqué techniques, but the one I recommend uses purchased paper-backed fusible web.

1. Trace or draw the shape to be appliquéd on the paper side of the fusible web, reversing the design if it's not symmetrical.

2. Fuse the web to the wrong side of the appliqué fabric.

3. Cut out the shape, remove the paper backing, and fuse the appliqué into place on the right side of the base fabric.

4. Stitch the appliqué edges with a satin zigzag stitch. For ease of stitching and the best finished appearance, use stabilizer (tissue paper or commercially available tear-away stabilizer) between the fabric and the sewing machine bed.

BANDING

A strip of fabric, folded under on one or both long edges, that is topstitched or fused to the face of the fabric.

BATTING

A layer of lightweight, lofty cotton or polyester non-woven material used to wrap, back, or pad a surface; sold off bolts or in quilt sizes.

BIAS STRIP

Fabric strip cut on the bias grain. When used for welting, bias strips are cut 1⅝ inches wide; when used to bind a hem or other edge, they're cut four times the desired finished width. They may also be used to make spaghetti ties. See also **Binding, Spaghetti Tie,** and **Welting,** in this section.

To Cut and Piece Separate Bias Strips

This method allows you to use all the fabric, but is more time-consuming than the method for creating continuous strips, which follows. Use cut-and-pieced strips when you need small quantities.

1. Plan to cut the strips four times finished width plus ¼ inch. Refer to the Bias Strip Yardage Chart, opposite, to determine the approximate running yardages.

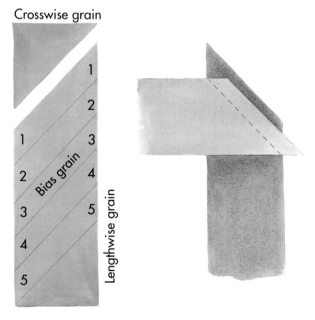

2. Fold the fabric diagonally so the lengthwise grain aligns with the crosswise grain. Press, then cut off the triangle along this fold.

3. Measure and mark lines parallel to the cut edge on both the triangle and the rest of the fabric, spacing the lines the desired bias width until you have as much as you need. If you have a rotary cutter, mat, and ruler, use them to speed the cutting process. Mark ¼-inch seam allowances along the lengthwise grain.

4. To join the strips in a continuous length: With right sides together, align two strips at a right angle, matching seamlines. Stitch and press the seams open. Trim off the extending points.

5. To speed the joining of separate bias strips, you can use the loop method, as shown in the illustration below. Align two strips at right angles, right sides together, matching seamlines. Stitch. Without lifting the presser foot, loop the end of the strip, right side up, close to the needle. Place a new strip right sides together at right angles. Continue to stitch straight across leaving two or three stitches before joining the next two strips. Once all the strips are joined, snip the threads between the individual seams.

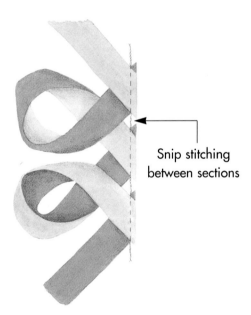

Snip stitching between sections

To Create Continuous Bias

This method is quicker than making separate bias strips, but it does not yield quite as much bias yardage because you cut away triangles at each end. Keep this in mind when referring to the Bias Strip Yardage Chart or when planning to piece the remaining triangles into strips as described in To Cut and Piece Separate Bias Strips.

1. Cut off a triangle and mark the fabric as described in Step 3 of the instructions for cutting and piecing strips. Cut off a mirror-image triangle at the opposite end of the fabric length.

2. On the wrong side of the fabric, number the strips with chalk or air-soluble marker, marking the same number at each end of the strip. With right sides together, form a tube by pinning the angled ends together, offsetting the ends by one strip width so Strip 1 extends beyond the seam end at one end and the strip with the highest number extends beyond the seam end at the other.

3. Stitch the edges in a ½-inch seam; press the seam open.

4. Cut continuous strips in a spiral by following the marked lines, starting between Strips 1 and 2.

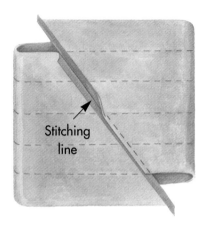

Stitching line

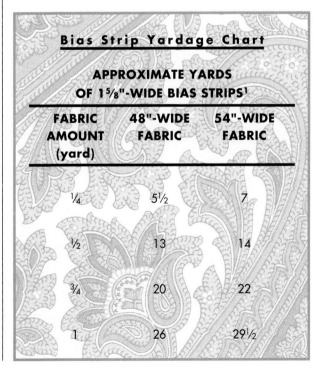

Bias Strip Yardage Chart

FABRIC AMOUNT (yard)	APPROXIMATE YARDS OF 1⅝"-WIDE BIAS STRIPS[1]	
	48"-WIDE FABRIC	54"-WIDE FABRIC
¼	5½	7
½	13	14
¾	20	22
1	26	29½

BINDING

A method of finishing a fabric edge to prevent raveling or to serve as a decorative accent. The method I recommend is the French binding (stitch-in-the-ditch) application.

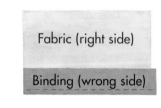

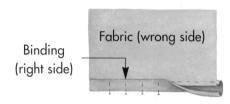

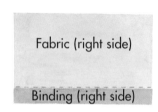

1. Placing right sides together, align the raw edge of the bias strip with the raw edge to be bound. Stitch the distance of the desired finished width away from the raw edges.

2. Bring the bias strip around to the wrong side, encasing the raw edge(s). Pin the binding in place so the other folded edge covers the previous stitching by at least ⅛ inch.

3. From the fabric right side, stitch in the "ditch" (the groove created where the binding joins the fabric), being sure to catch the binding on the wrong side.

To Finish Binding Ends

1. Apply the first edge of the binding to the fabric, extending the binding ¾ inch beyond the fabric edge. Trim the fabric seam allowance at the corner on the diagonal.

2. Fold the extending end of the binding back onto itself, then fold the binding down over the fabric edge and complete the application, pivoting to sew across the open end.

To Join Binding Ends

1. To seam binding ends, start the binding application 2 inches from the beginning point, allowing an extra 1½ inches of binding. Stop the binding application 2 inches from the other side of the beginning point, again allowing an extra 1½ inches of binding.

2. Trim the binding ends on the diagonal, leaving ½-inch seam allowance on each end, and stitch them with right sides together.

3. Press the seams open and continue stitching the binding into place.

CLEAN-FINISHING

Techniques used to finish raw edges: zigzagging, serging, pinking, or binding with fabric strips.

CLIPPING

Snipping into the seam allowances on a curved seam to allow them to lie smooth. (See also **Notching,** in this section.) Clipping may also be used for marking and matching.

CORNER

To create smooth, strong corners, use these techniques:

1. On inside corners, stop stitching at the turning point and leave the needle lowered into the fabric. Raise the presser foot and turn the fabric, aligning with the adjoining seamline. Lower the presser foot and continue stitching.

2. To join an inward corner to an outward corner, reinforce the inward corner (see **Reinforcing,** in this section). Clip up to the reinforced stitches. Spread the clipped area so it fits the other edge; pin into place. With the clipped side up, stitch on the seamline, pivoting the fabric at the corner.

DART

A method of controlling fullness at curved edges. During pin-fitting, pin fabric layers together up to the curved area. Then, working from the center out, form one or more narrow, equal-sided darts in the longer fabric edge to fit it to the shorter edge. Pin the darts into place. Chalk the dartlines on the wrong side of the fabric, marking over the pins. Remove pins. Refold the dart, right sides together, matching markings. Pin and stitch, sewing from the fabric edge to the dart tip; shorten the stitch length as you come to the tip. Trim the dart allowance to ¼ inch.

DIAGONAL BASTING

A handstitch used for holding layers of fabric and/or batting together. Take short stitches through the fabric at a right angle to the edge, spacing them evenly. The stitches on the top will be diagonal and those on the underside will be horizontal.

DOUBLE-CUTTING

A method of cutting two sides or two sections of a slipcover simultaneously; used in cases where the furniture is identical on both sides. Double-cutting can be a real time-saver when working with inside and outside arms, front arm panels, and shoulder panels. To use this method:

1. Block out the sections as originally instructed, planning a left and right side. The pin-fitting method also proceeds as usual except that you will fit and trim two pieces at the same time.

2. With either the two right sides or the two wrong sides together, pin the layers on one side of the slipcover. Pin closely and carefully, then mark the exact stitching line on both layers. Trim the seams as usual. Use notches and clips generously and chalk-mark the location of the seam intersection. Unpin and separate the layers, then repin them to the appropriate sides.

DROP

The distance from the top of a piece of furniture to the floor, rug, or other desired lower position.

EASE

A technique for joining two slightly different lengths of fabric, usually along a curve. Excess fullness is worked into the seamline without the use of gathers, tucks, or darts by manipulating the fibers, stretching the shorter side and crowding the longer.

ENLARGING PATTERNS AND DIAGRAMS

A method of converting patterns represented on a small grid to actual size.

1. Draw on a piece of paper a large grid of squares whose size is equal to that marked on the pattern grid (usually 1 inch) or buy 1-inch grid paper at an office- or art-supply store.

2. Copy the pattern freehand, one square at a time, onto the large grid.

Note: In some cases, if the full-sized pattern will not be too large, you may be able to use a copy machine to enlarge your patterns.

FOLDS

A method of controlling fullness; working from the center out, form small, equal creases until the larger edge fits the smaller fabric edge.

GATHERING

The process of creating soft, even pleats so a length of fabric fills a smaller distance across. The fullness of the gathers is determined by the fabric, but usually the length of the piece is 1½ to 3 times the distance to be spanned, with 2 times being the average. To gather, select one of the following methods:

Straight-Stitch Method

1. Using a long, loose machine stitch, make two parallel rows of gathering stitches. Position the first row along the seamline in the seam allowance and the second ¼ inch closer to the raw edge. To avoid thread breakage, use extra-strength thread in the bobbin and a loose upper tension.

2. Anchor the threads at one end of the stitching.

3. Pull gently on the bobbin thread until the correct length is reached. Anchor the thread. Adjust the gathers by sliding the fabric along the threads.

Zigzag Method

1. Using a long, wide zigzag stitch, sew over a strong, thin string ⅛ inch above the seamline, carefully avoiding sewing into the string.

2. Secure one end of the string. Pull up the other end of the string and adjust the gathers evenly.

3. Stitch the gathers in place. Remove the string.

Ruffler Method

This method requires a ruffler attachment suitable for your machine. This attachment gathers automatically with each stitch. Test-stitch on fabric scraps, adjusting the ruffler's screw mechanism and the stitch length to produce the desired degree of ruffling.

Serger Differential Feed Method

This method requires a serger (overlock) machine with differential feed feature. This feature utilizes two sets of feed dogs (front and back) that work together at the same or different rates. In a "plus setting," the front feed dogs take in more fabric than the back feed dogs release, causing gathering. Test-serge on fabric scraps, adjusting the differential feed to a higher plus setting for more gathering. You may also want to lengthen the stitch, to allow for more gathering under the stitch, and/or tighten the needle tension.

MITERING

A method of shaping slipcovers where a continuous piece of fabric must shape to fit a corner. To create a miter, pin the fabric to each side of the corner, then smooth the fabric to a point at the corner; pin along the corner and trim the excess fabric.

MUSLIN

A sample of a finished project made in an inexpensive fabric so adjustments can be made in the pattern pieces before being cut from expensive fabric. Also, any of a variety of plain-weave cotton fabrics from which samples are often made.

NOTCHING

Cutting small wedges from the seam allowances on inward curves to allow seams to lie smoothly and eliminate bulk. See also **Clipping,** in this section. Notching may also be used for marking and matching.

PRESHRINKING

Treating a fabric by using the cleaning method intended for the finished project. This important step will allow any substantial shrinkage to occur before a project is made. See also Prepare—Preshrink!, on page 16.

QUILTING

A means of holding two layers of fabric and one of batting together in a decorative fashion. Allow about 10 percent extra fabric in length and width for quilting take-up. Sandwich and pin the batting between the wrong sides of the face fabric and lining piece. Sew along drawn design lines. See also French Chair, page 67.

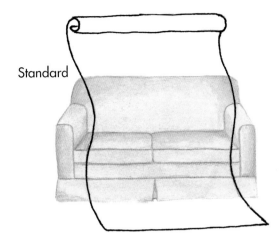

Standard

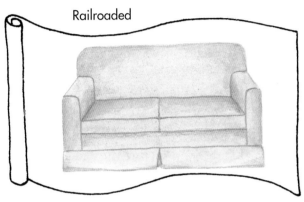

Railroaded

RAILROADING

Aligning patterns along the fabric width (horizontally) instead of along the fabric length (vertically). This method is usually used to eliminate or reduce seams or to follow a specific design line. However, using this method can affect the stretch and recover capabilities of the slipcover, because the vertical threads—those with less give—will be positioned around the furniture. Also, residual shrinking is more likely to occur along those vertical threads, which may cause the laundered slipcover to fit improperly.

REINFORCING

Strengthening a seam area by sewing with short stitches $\frac{1}{16}$ inch from the seamline, within the seam allowance. This is usually done for short distances on either side of a potentially weak area, such as where seam allowances will be clipped, notched, or trimmed close to the seamline.

REPEAT

One complete pattern on a print or woven fabric. To determine the size of a repeat, measure the distance from one point in the design to the next identical point. If the fabric has a repeat larger than 3 inches, you'll need to add extra yardage to allow for centering motifs on each cushion and panel. To calculate the exact yardage needed when using a fabric with a large repeat, figure yardage for each slipcover section separately. To estimate safely, allow an extra repeat for each slipcover section to be centered.

SELVAGE

The finished edge that runs along both sides of the fabric length to prevent raveling. Do not use these as seam allowances—they may cause puckering.

SLIP-BASTING

Used during the matching process to hold fabric in place while you stitch. Press under the upper layer of the fabric, along the seamline. Lap the pressed-under edge over the other section, matching the design along the lower layer's proposed seamline. Pin. Baste the two layers together by inserting the needle through the fold in the upper layer, then through the lower section, making the stitches on each layer about ¼ inch long. Open out the seam allowance and stitch along the basting.

SPAGHETTI TIE

A narrow fabric tube used as a tie to hold two fabric edges together or to secure a decorative cover to furniture. To make spaghetti ties, cut straight- or bias-grain fabric strips the length needed by twice the desired finished width plus seam allowances.

• **FOR TUBULAR TIES.** Fold the strips in half lengthwise, right sides together, and sew them along the long edge and across one end. Leave the seam allowances untrimmed to fill the tube. Turn using a tube-turning tool available at your fabric store or via mail-order sources. Do not press the ties. *Note:* A tube turner allows you to insert a filler inside the tube.

• **FOR FLAT TIES.** Press the long raw edges into the strip center, then press the strip in half lengthwise, turning in the raw ends. Edgestitch along all edges.

TASSEL

A tuft of loosely hanging threads or cord. For instructions on creating tassels, see Making Your Own Tassel Ties, on page 28.

TEMPLATE

A pattern that reflects the exact size and shape of an object. To make a template, measure the greatest width and depth of the seat, back, or arm and cut a piece of newspaper or kraft paper a little larger. Lay the paper over the surface, folding or chalk-marking the exact outline, clipping and folding as needed to accommodate arms or back supports. Cut out this shape and check its accuracy by laying it on the surface once more; adjust if necessary. After the exact size and shape are determined, make a new pattern, adding the necessary seam allowances. If your piece of furniture has a shape that is difficult to cover, use a piece of muslin to make the template.

WELTING

Fabric-wrapped cord, also called piping or cording, used to define or finish seams, to give seams added strength, and to add a decorative touch. To create good-looking welting, cover purchased $\frac{5}{32}$- to ¼-inch-diameter cotton cording with bias strips (see **Bias Strip,** earlier in this section) cut from the desired fabric. Methods of creating and working with welting follow.

To Create Welting

1. Wrap the strip, right side out, around the cord so the raw edges are even.

2. Using a zipper foot positioned to the right of the needle, stitch next to the cord, but do not crowd it.

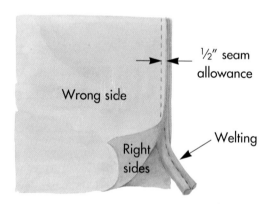

To Apply Welting

1. Position the welting on the right side of a slipcover section to be welted, with the stitching on the seamline; baste the welting into place within the seam allowances, ⅛ inch from the stitching.

2. When catching the welting in a seam, sandwich the welting between the layers, with the prewelted layer on top. Stitch just inside the welting stitching, as close as possible to the cording.

3. At seam intersections where welting crosses welting, remove 1 inch of cord from the welting ends. Try to anticipate seams where this will happen so you can prepare the welting ahead of time.

To Turn Corners and Curves with Welting

• **FOR A VERY SQUARE CORNER.** In the welting seam allowance, clip close to the stitching line at the corner point.

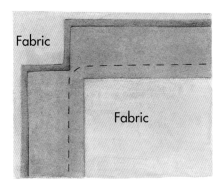

• **FOR A SLIGHTLY CURVED CORNER.** Make 1½-inch clips in the welting seam allowance on each side of the corner point.

• **ON OTHER CURVED AREAS.** In the welting seam allowance, clip as needed to make the welting lie flat.

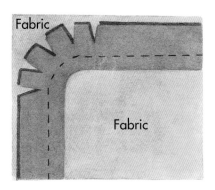

To Butt Welting Ends

1. Plan welting joins so they are at inconspicuous locations. At the beginning of a welting strip, leave about ½ inch unstitched; at the end, stop stitching about 1½ inches from the beginning point.

2. Trim the end of the welting so the beginning and end overlap about 1 inch. Open the welting stitching along the 1½-inch unstitched end area, and trim the cording so it butts the other end.

3. At the end of the welting, fold under the extending fabric about ½ inch. Wrap it over the other end to make a smooth join.

4. Complete the stitching; be sure to backstitch at the beginning.

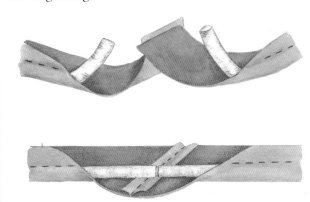

To Cross Welted Seams

Try to anticipate where welted seams will cross. Before sewing the seams, prepare the welting as described in these steps:

1. Trim the welting ends flush with the raw edge of the fabric.

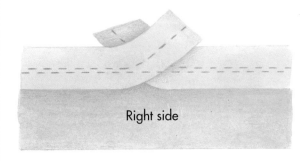

2. Pull out and cut off 1 inch of the cord at the welting end; smooth the casing.

To Clean-Finish Welting at an Opening

Where welting will end at an opening, such as the zipper closure area:

1. Allow the welting to extend beyond the raw edge at the opening, then remove about 1½ inches of the welting stitching.

2. Cut the cord even with the seamline, leaving the bias strip intact.

3. Wrap the bias strip back over the cord and restitch the welting into place.

4. Complete the finishing process for the opening.

Resource Guide

FABRICS

Boussac of France
979 Third Avenue
New York, NY 10022
(212) 421-0534
Pages 26, 27, 30, 60, 80, 83, 87

Brunschwig & Fils
979 Third Avenue
New York, NY 10022
(212) 838-7878
Through architects and interior designers. Cover and pages 2, 9, 10, 14, 15, 22, 24, 25, 34, 57, 58, 60, 62, 64, 66, 67, 92, 93, 96

Calico Corners
203 Gale Lane
Kennett Square, PA 19348
(800) 821-7700 ext. 810
Call for nearest retail outlet. Large seller of decorative fabrics.

Clarence House
979 Third Avenue
New York, NY 10022
(212) 752-2890
Through architects and interior designers. Pages 34, 35, 63, 76

Covington Fabric
15 East 26th Street
New York, NY 10010
(212) 689-2200
Pages 1, 9, 17, 20, 22, 33, 36, 39, 50, 52, 54, 56, 57, 58, 60, 61, 62, 88, 95, 98

Cyrus Clark
267 Fifth Avenue
New York, NY 10016
(212) 684-5312
Pages 5, 6, 7, 12, 24, 34, 55, 84

The Fabric Center
485 Electric Avenue
PO Box 8212
Fitchburg, MA 01420
(508) 343-4402
Mail-order source with discounts on many decorative fabrics.

Hancock Fabrics
Mail Order Department
3841 Hinkleville Road
Paducah, KY 42001
(800) 552-9255
Mail-order source for home decorating fabric, sewing notions, and Conso trims and decorating products.

Payne
979 Third Avenue
New York, NY 10022
(800) 543-4322
Page 33

Schumacher
79 Madison Avenue
New York, NY 10016
(800) 552-9255
Through architects and interior designers. Pages 4, 13, 26, 28, 32, 33, 53, 54, 72, 106

Springs Industries
Ultrafabrics Division
104 West 40th Street
New York, NY 10018
(800) 633-8870
Pages 46, 60, 90, 91

Waverly
79 Madison Avenue
New York, NY 10016
(800) 423-5881
Through architects, interior designers, and select retail stores. Pages 18, 24, 87

Westpoint Stevens Home Fashions
1185 Sixth Avenue
New York, NY 10036
(800) 533-8229
Pages 18, 24, 78

FURNITURE

Beachley Furniture Company
227 North Prospect Street
Hagerstown, MD 21741-0978
(800) 344-1887 or (301) 733-1910
Cover and pages 15, 20, 22, 32, 39, 50, 64, 75

Crate and Barrel
(800) 249-4158
Call for the store nearest you. Pages 92, 93, 95

The Door Store
1 Park Avenue
New York, NY 10016
(800) 433-4071
Pages 2, 10, 30, 67, 69, 80, 107

Southwood Furniture Corporation
2860 Nathan Street
Hickory, NC 28603
(800) 345-1777
Pages 12, 13, 53, 54, 55, 70, 72, 106

Stessl and Neugebauer
9 Industrial Place
Summit, NJ 07901
(908) 277-3340
Page 87

Make It with Style: Slipcovers

TRIMS AND NOTIONS

Blumenthal/Lansing Co.
Lansing, IA 52151
(212) 752-2535
Buttons available at fine
fabric and craft stores.
Pages 35, 63

Clotilde, Inc.
2 Sew Smart Way
B8031
Stevens Point, WI
54481-8031
(800) 772-2891
Mail-order source for
sewing notions.

CM Offray & Son, Inc.
Route 24, Box 601
Chester, NJ 07930
(908) 879-4700
Major source for ribbons
and ribbon trims. Pages
26, 27, 30, 35, 76, 80, 83

Coats & Clark's Sales
Corporation
30 Patewood Drive
Suite 351
Greenville, SC 29615
(800) 241-5997
Manufacturer of bias
bindings.

Conso Products
PO Box 326
Union, SC 29379
(800) 845-2431
Major manufacturer of
trims and home decorating
and sewing notions.

DMC Thread
10 Port Kearney
South Kearney, NJ
07032-4688
(201) 589-0606
Pages 10, 25, 27, 96

Freudenberg
Nonwovens
Pellon Consumer
Products
3440 Industrial Drive
Durham, NC 27704
(800) 223-5275
Pellon products are
available in home-sewing
and crafts stores across
North America. Pages 6,
7, 60, 84, 88

M & J Trimming
1014 Sixth Avenue
New York, NY 10018
(212) 391-6200 or
391-8731
Pages 9, 10, 18, 24, 25, 57,
64, 78, 87, 96, 106

Prym-Dritz Corporation
PO Box 5028
Spartanburg, SC 29304
(800) 845-4948
Major manufacturer of
trims, grommets, and
notions. Pages 75, 80, 83,
95, 101

SHS Custom Embroidery
362 Springfield Avenue
Summit, NJ 07901
(908) 522-0580
Pages 48, 50, 78

Wrights
Manufacturer of bias
binding and twill tapes.
Found at any fine fabric
store.

WORKROOMS

All slipcovers and
interior design by
Donna Lang LTD
180 Main Street
Chatham, NJ 07928
(973) 635-4805

Mavis Brown
Chatham, NJ 07928
Page 24

Chester Herbert
636 Thomas Boulevard
East Orange, NJ 07017
(201) 672-6887
Cover and pages 12, 13,
32, 33, 50, 52, 53, 64, 70,
72, 75, 87, 98

Casey Pervis
Gulfport, MS 39507
Pages 1, 9, 76

Judith A. Petersen
Enterprises
19 Sherman Avenue
Summit, NJ 07901
(908) 277-3994
Cover and pages 2, 5, 6, 7,
10, 15, 22, 30, 67, 69, 78,
80, 83, 84, 88, 90, 91, 92,
93, 95, 96

Shirley Westcott
Gulfport, MS 39507
Pages 1, 9, 22, 35, 76

Index